BEYOND THE BOTTOM LINE

BEYOND THE BOTTOM LINE

Alan Warner

First published 1992 by Gower Publishing Company Limited, Aldershot, Hampshire.

This paperback edition published 1993 by
Gower Publishing
Gower House
Croft Road
Aldershot
Hants GU11 3HR
England

Gower
Old Post Road
Brookfield
Vermont 05036
USA

Reprinted 1995

CIP catalogue records for this book are avaialbe from the British Library

ISBN 0 566 07479 6

Typeset in 11 point Plantin by QT Associates
and printed in Great Britain by Hartnoll's Ltd, Bodmin

Preface

This book and its predecessor *The Bottom Line* could only have been produced with the assistance of people who are very close to me.

I would particularly like to thank my family – Jenny, Helen, Angela and Anthony – for their tolerance and for their story line ideas; some may have been bizarre but many others were implemented!

I would also like to thank Heather and Cathcrine for their efforts in producing the typed manuscript; Jill Whitelam, John Guiniven and John Rothenburg for their advice on technical issues in the first part of the book; and my Partners and other work colleagues who were supportive and tolerant of my time commitment.

These colleagues have also contributed much to the concepts and ideas contained in the second part of the book because we are all on a constant learning curve when developing the scope of financial concepts.

I hope this book helps others to join us.

Alan Warner

Summary of Content

PART ONE: Fighting off the Predator

Directors considering a potential acquisition, including the relevance of investor relations and asset values (tangible and intangible) to share price.

PART TWO: Fighting for Survival

ix

PART ONE

FIGHTING OFF THE PREDATOR

Chapter 1

I'm sitting in my boss's office, looking morosely across the desk at him, the man who's largely been responsible for making the last four years the happiest of my working life. We're discussing the fax which arrived at our New Jersey offices in such a routine way this morning, a fax which seems likely to throw both our careers off the rails. "I just can't believe it Phil," says Richard. "I know we always accepted that we might get taken over but Universal! I couldn't stand working for them again."

I remember that Richard always found Universal's culture and control systems much too stultifying. That was why he left them to come back to the States and become Company President of Chapman Foods. I wasn't so desperate to leave Universal but Richard made me an offer I couldn't refuse. And I had my own reasons for wanting to leave Britain for a new start. It was my only chance of getting my family together again.

As Richard rings his secretary to ask, for the fourth time, if she's heard when the Chairman of the Board will be arriving, my mind wanders back to the way my move to the US has changed my life and how great it really has been, until today that is. My marriage is mended, my relationship with Jean better than ever, my kids well balanced (if slightly too American for my liking) and we have a standard of living better than anything I dreamed of during my days with Lawrensons and Universal. And I'm good at my job, now confirmed as Vice President, Sales and Marketing and effectively Richard's number two.

"He's just arrived Phil," says Richard. "He wants just us two in the Boardroom. He says we'll see the other VPs later."

We leave Richard's office and make for the lift to the top floor. As we go into the outer office, Karen, Richard's secretary, looks at him and me with an expression which sums up her total devastation at the news. She's been at Chapmans for over twenty years and, as far as we can tell, it seems to be her whole life. She's the only other person who knows yet and we are sure that she'll keep quiet. She's that sort of secretary.

The Chairman, Miles Chapman the Third, is standing behind the Board Room table, gazing out of the window. Miles is in his late thirties and has the difficult task of following in Father and Grandfather's footsteps when maybe he hasn't got the flair or the drive which were behind their success in building up the business. He was sent to Harvard to get his MBA but I always feel he'd rather be painting pictures, something which he seems to do in every possible moment of his spare time. But still he does a good job, particularly at managing the conflicting interests of the many family members who hold shares. But the bid from Universal could be much more difficult to manage than anything he's had to cope with before.

He greets us with a smile which doesn't extend to his eyes. He appears to be under strain and I think to myself that he looks how I feel. He ushers us to sit down with him at the end of the huge Boardroom table. Richard on one side of him, me on the other.

Miles is fairhaired with glasses and a fresh complexion, looking much younger than he really is. He belongs to a different generation from Richard and me – we are both in our late forties.

"OK you two," he says. "Let's see what these British bastards are up to."

He remembers where I came from and quickly says, "Sorry Phil – I was forgetting you're British too."

"No problem Miles," I say, pleased that you can be

informal even with the Company Chairman in the US. "Think of me as adopted – I'm certainly on this side of the Atlantic for this battle."

"You see a battle then," says Miles. "What makes you believe that?"

I realise that he's caught me out and quickly try to get out of it.

"I was assuming that the family would fight the bid but I accept that it's too early to assume that. I'm sorry."

Richard gives me a look across the table which says 'Hard luck pal, be more careful next time' and I try to return a look which says I will.

Miles carries on, "I think you're probably right. Many of my relations won't want to sell and there'll be an emotional reaction against a British company. But everyone has their price and a lot will depend on the reaction of the other shareholders. The external holdings are about fifty-five per cent now and they'll sell if the deal is right. Tell me the price again."

Richard looks at me because I manage the financial side for him. This still seems amazing to me when I remember that five years ago I didn't even know the difference between a Profit & Loss Account and a Balance Sheet. But that was before I met a young woman who changed my life and now happens to be in the US too, carving out a career for herself in Wall Street.

Nevertheless my financial knowledge still has many limitations but, based on my experience at Lawrensons, I have been able to contribute a lot to the development of better control information which Richard and I need to run this business. Until three months ago I was supported by Mel Munnings, a superb Chief Financial Officer who was my right-hand man and a very competent operator in the areas of treasury and external reporting where I am still very weak.

Mel was then headhunted to a big electronics company on the West Coast and, despite the best efforts of New York's top selection agencies, we still haven't replaced him. So, for the time being, I'm left with a 'Controller', as they're called over here, who used to be responsible to Mel for the routine planning and reporting function and who has been holding the fort for me until a replacement is found.

My experience of this kind of thing is confined to reading the FT and the Wall Street Journal – I know little about acquisitions and the financial complexity which surrounds them. I make this point to Miles.

"OK Phil, I hear what you say and we'll get some expert advice right away. But tell me what you do know."

"Well, our price was $40 yesterday and it's not moved recently so there were no pre-bid rumours. This bid from Universal is $51 which values the business at $500 million."

"Mmm," says Miles, "that's more than I expected. It's well placed – enough to be tempting. How does it compare with the Balance Sheet values?"

"Way over Miles," I reply, "Net Assets are only $180 million. But they don't really count – it's our brands they're after. Universal always go for strong brands and they're not shown in the Balance Sheet because we've never bought them."

"Too right," intervenes Richard, the emotion showing in his voice, "but we've sweated blood to build them up these last four years and now Universal want to walk in and pick them up."

"OK you guys," says Miles, "let's just cool it. We've got a lot to think about. When did they say they're releasing this?"

"They're putting out a press release in the UK about now, 2 o'clock their time," says Richard, "so we need a holding statement for the shareholders and a response for the press. And we need to decide when and how we tell the staff."

"Richard, you go and start the arrangements to announce it to the staff. Leave it about an hour before you make the first statement and check with me that the other releases have already gone out," says Miles decisively. "Tell them the truth, don't promise them anything you can't deliver and say we will do all we can to protect their interests. And send Mike Westwood in as you go out – I'll have to brief him about precisely what we're going to say to the press and the shareholders. Phil you stay here because we've got to get some outside help in – and quickly."

As Richard gets up to leave, I note the calm authority which Miles has assumed. Maybe I've underestimated him all along. I'm curious as to how Richard is going to tell all our 8000 employees in seven different locations but that's his problem.

Mike Westwood, our Public Relations Manager, comes in breathless and soon Miles is agreeing the text of the statements. We decide to say very little – just that the approach is being considered and that the Directors will recommend what is in the interests of all the shareholders. As Miles and Mike are discussing the final wording, I think more about Miles's comment on external advice. He's absolutely right – we're just not geared up to cope with something like this. Even First National, the Investment Bank we've used for our previous external work – like the new issue of capital two years ago – are not known as one of the big names in acquisition advice. It's becoming an increasingly specialised area.

It suddenly dawns on me how ridiculously under-prepared we are. We should have had an action plan in place and the best advisers briefed. Now we're all running around like headless chickens and it won't look good to the outside world unless we can act quickly and decisively.

As Mike Westwood scurries out with the text we've agreed to release, Miles turns to me and says "Right Phil, get on the phone to Henry Mears while I start to contact the other external Board Members. I'm not sure if I can get hold of many of them – they're all over the country right now."

Henry is President of First National and I know he's a friend of the Chapman family. I know it's going to be tough to change Miles's mind, but I decide to try.

"Are you sure we should use First National, Miles?" I ask. "They're not specialists at this sort of thing and you said we needed the best advice. It can make all the difference."

Miles looks at me quizzically and I find it hard to guess

what he's thinking. Have I overstepped the mark? After about 30 seconds silence he replies, "You're right Phil, find out the name of those guys who've just left Manhattan Trust and set up their own outfit. I've heard they're shit hot. And we'll need the best legal backup too. I'll speak to one of my friends about that – he knows them all and he'll give me independent advice."

"OK Miles," I say, not knowing how on earth I can find these acquisition specialists from his vague description. "Anything else I can do now?"

"No, I don't think so. There's nothing much we can do until I've got the Board together and I'm trying for this evening. I'll want you to organise some kind of presentation of the financials so you'd better get moving."

As I walk out the door, my mind is in a whirl. How can someone like me, who in the UK was an ordinary Sales and Marketing Director, suddenly be making a presentation to the Board of a major US corporation about a multi-million acquisition?

The feeling I get is a combination of terror and elation. I know from my past experience of learning about financial matters that anything is possible once you have the confidence to break through the jargon and the mystique. But you also need someone to help you, as I had those years ago in the UK when that young woman revived my career and changed my life.

I must not waste time. I need the best advice – and quickly.

Chapter 2

As I rush back to my office, my secretary Tracy says, "Phil, Jean's on the phone."

I'm surprised that Tracy hasn't told her I'm too busy in view of this morning's drama, although I'm not sure if Tracy knows yet. I'm just going to say I'll ring her back when I remember why our marriage broke up all those years ago. Because I got too obsessed with work and forgot my family.

I go into my office and pick up the phone. "Hi love," I say, "we've got great drama here today so I'll have to be quick."

I think she might ask about the drama but she doesn't – she's obviously worried about something.

"Phil, I've just had Angie on the phone. There's a meeting about her High School options and it's this evening. She never told us which is typical of her. But there's nothing in the diary so can we go together, about seven?"

"Darling, I'd love to but it's impossible. That drama I mentioned – it's serious. Universal have made an approach to buy Chapmans and there's a Board Meeting tonight. I'm really sorry but I just can't go."

"I see," she says. "Alright, I'll go myself – this seems to have a familiar ring to me. I thought you'd changed since you came over here."

"Darling," I reply, hardly believing my ears. "Did you

hear what I said? Universal are trying to take us over. Do you know what that could mean?"

There's a few seconds silence and I hope she's thinking again. I'm relieved when she replies "Sorry love, it didn't really register first time. Will they take Chapmans over?"

"It's too early to say yet love. I'll try to ring you later. Hope the meeting is OK."

"Thanks darling. I love you."

I say I love her too and I think how nice those words sound after all those bitter years we had apart. I found relief in work and womanising while Jean devoted herself to the children. I didn't deserve to get her back but now I've got her I won't make the same mistake again.

I keep the phone in my hand and buzz for Tracy. "Tracy, find me the last four weeks' copies of the Wall Street Journal and ask Carl to come in here right away." I suddenly remember that Tracy may still not know the news. "Oh and pop in here for a minute please."

Tracy comes in and I ask her to sit down. She's a sweet woman who's been with me ever since I came over here. She was straight out of High School then but now she's grown into a highly competent secretary who makes my life at Chapmans so easy. Before I changed my ways I'd no doubt have been chasing her like I chased all the other secretaries because she's a gorgeously attractive brunette. But she's getting married shortly and I've been concerned that she might leave to have a baby. I think that such matters seem so trivial now that Universal are trying to take us over and I'm facing a crucial Board Meeting tonight.

"Tracy," I say, "has Richard told you some important news this morning?"

"Yes Phil," she replies, "he called me into Karen's office when he came down from the Board Room."

"Where is he now?"

"He's in the main factory, talking to the managers. He's trying to arrange for all the Site Managers to tell their people at about the same time."

"Right. Now it's going to be quite a day, Tracy, quite a few weeks I expect. Try to pass all my routine mail and messages to either Jane or Henry. Get those Wall Street

Journals and show Carl in as you go. Could you try to stay close to your desk because I may need you to get me calls any time."

"Sure Phil. I'll be around. Aren't I always?"

She gives me a lovely smile as she leaves my office. I think how competent and well balanced these young American women seem to be. None of the scattiness of their counterparts in the UK, more concerned with office politics and what was on TV the previous night.

A moment later Carl Palinski walks through my door. Carl's my Controller who is reporting to me for all the financial side of the business until I find a new CFO. He's a good man – solid and reliable but hardly inspiring. He's done all the accounting examinations that are required over here but has little imagination and creativity and we always seem to have to push him to produce any new initiatives on the management accounting side. I'm not sure what his experience of acquisitions has been but I fear it's as little as mine. He's been at Chapman's over ten years and he's still under forty.

He looks worried and flustered but I recall that this is his normal response to anything out of his daily routine. I ask him to sit down.

"OK Carl, we've got quite a day on our hands and I want you to drop everything else. First of all, tell me what you know."

"Only that Universal of the UK have made a bid for us and the Board are meeting as soon as possible. That's all Richard told me."

"That's almost all there is pal," I say, "except the price. Fifty-one dollars valuing us at 500 million."

Carl thinks for a while but makes no comment and I suspect that he's feeling as insecure as I am.

I carry on. "Now, we've got to get in some top financial advice. Miles suggested some guys who left Manhattan Trust recently to go out on their own. Any idea who they are?"

Carl looks down with a pained expression on his face. "I know who you mean Phil. Three names, the last one is Italian I'm sure. I'd know it if you told me."

Tracy walks in with an armful of newspapers and we begin to scan the headlines. It only takes a few minutes before Carl says, "Here it is! Faber, Kensley and Benetto. Apparently Manhattan Trust are suing them."

"Never mind that," I say, "how do we find them?"

Ten minutes later we've found the address and I'm speaking to Mr Benetto's PA. I explain the position and she asks me to hang on.

"Can I help you Mr Moorley?" says a confident voice. "I'm Paul Benetto. I guess you're ringing about Universal's bid. We hoped you might call."

"I sure am," I say, thinking how easily I've picked up the American ways of saying things. "Can you get over here right away? There's a Board Meeting tonight and I need a briefing. I may want one of you to be there."

He makes a token attempt to check his availability but I know he's going to come. This is the sort of high profile bid which is going to get them established – provided they are on the right side of course.

He says he'll be over within two hours – I look at my watch and see it's 11.30am. I now find myself in the ridiculous position of not knowing what to do next. I send Carl away to work out all he can on the financial implications and then find that there is no mail, no messages and no telephone calls – because of my clear instructions to Tracy. I telephone Miles to tell him about Benetto and he asks me to arrange for Benetto to see him with me and Richard about 4 pm. He also tells me that there will be a Board Meeting at 7.30 pm. I decide I'd better find Richard and tell him what I've done. We always work together so well and tell each other everything. Universal aren't going to change that.

As I leave my office, I almost bump into him as he rushes back to his own. He asks me to follow him and I try, without success, to keep pace with his retreating figure. I contrast this with Richard's normal relaxed approach to his job and I realise how Universal really have changed our lives. I find it hard to believe that things will ever be the same again.

Chapter 3

I'm sitting in the Board Room for the second time today
and this time it's full. Miles is at the head of the table,
listening intently to Paul Benetto as he tells us some
hometruths about the Universal bid. Four other members
of the Chapman family are present, including Miles's father
who, the gossip says, still has to approve every major
decision. There are also three non-executive Board
Members, all well-known top executives from other
companies, and there are the three Executive Vice
Presidents – John Madden in charge of Production, Al
Morton, Personnel and me. Then there's Carl who
combines his Controller responsibilities with keeping the
minutes of Board Meetings. Finally there's Richard who's
sitting between Miles and Benetto near the end of the table
and I can tell from the expression on his face that he's
hating every moment of this. Richard is great as an
Executive President but he's not cut out for anything other
than running a business. That's why he left Universal – he
was spending too much time on managing the bureaucracy
and the company politics.
   This Benetto is quite an operator and I'm highly
impressed. From the moment he entered my office about
six hours ago, I knew I was going to like him. He's tall,
dark, good looking in a Latin sort of way and he has a
combination of charm and confidence which immediately
sent Tracy into a spin. But, after half an hour with him, I

realised that he has an impressive brain too.

Our early discussion confirmed my insecurity about handling the financial implications of the deal. He talked about earnings multiples, exit multiples and prospective multiples in a way which left me completely floored. I reminded him that I wasn't too clued up on the detail of acquisitions as Chapmans' policy has always been to grow organically. For a few minutes he slowed down slightly but I was still out of my depth. There just wasn't time for me to ask him to explain the basic principles and I privately resolved that I must do something about it later.

We met Miles at 4 pm and Richard was there too, a combination of anger, boredom and frustration on his face. Benetto told us what he is now telling the Board. That the offer is well placed; an excess of over 25% on yesterday's market price, a price/earnings multiple of 15 (and a prospective multiple of 13 whatever that means) with an option to take either cash or the equivalent in Universal shares. His view was that the non-family shareholders would be highly unlikely to turn it down unless there was an alternative offer from what he called a 'White Knight'.

He also said that, despite these facts, he believed that Universal might go higher if necessary because they wanted Chapmans very badly. They had bid for two companies in the US during the last eighteen months and both had been narrowly lost to a competitor.

My mind comes back to the present as Benetto makes this same point to the Board. There have been no questions so far but now one of the external non-executive directors chips in, "But Mr Benetto. How are Universal going to justify this to their shareholders? You're talking about a post-tax multiple of 15 which you say they will increase. How much, in your judgement?"

"Difficult to say but 18 maybe even 20."

"But that will cripple their profitability. A multiple of 20 means a yield of 5% on capital invested. It's bound to affect their EPS in a big way."

"You're right, sir," replies Benetto, "but there are special factors. Remember the British write off goodwill straight to reserves so there's no charge against earnings as there would be for a US company. And I reckon they must be looking for substantial synergy with their other US food operations."

I look round the table and see a row of faces. Some looking puzzled, some concerned. I'm not surprised. I haven't a clue what that conversation was all about until the last bit. Synergy. I heard all about that when I was with Universal. Two plus two equals five. Savings achieved from combining two companies – production, distribution, selling, research – savings achieved by closing down factories and rationalising operations, savings achieved by ditching people who've given their working lives to the company. I also remember that Universal tend to impose their stamp on new acquisitions by stripping out top management, closing down Head Offices and putting their own people in key positions. I shudder inwardly at the prospect.

Meanwhile Benetto is spelling out the options. I'm impressed that he has these on an OHP transparency despite the short time he has had to prepare. It reads like this:

SHAREHOLDER OPTIONS

- Accept what is, fundamentally, a good offer.
- Reject the offer as insufficient and hope that they will come back with more.
- Reject the offer and hope for a White Knight.
- Reject the offer and approach potential White Knights.
- Consult lawyers for possible legal defence options.

"But Mr Benetto," says Miles's father George, "how can we justify recommending rejection? What will be our argument to our other shareholders?"

"I could help you with a good defence, sir. I'd need to study your asset portfolio and look at the market prices of your real estate. And we could bring the brands into it. A lot of European companies are bringing brands into their Balance Sheets by new methods of valuation. We could also look at your future profit projections and see what we can do with those. Our argument would be that the company is worth more."

"I'd prefer to concentrate on the lack of strategic fit," intervenes Richard, speaking for the first time. "There is very little logic in merging the US operations of the two companies. It just makes no sense at all."

I think Richard may be allowing his antipathy towards Universal to affect his usually superb marketing judgement. But I'm surprised at Benetto's strong and immediate rejection of his arguments.

"You may be right Mr Watts, but I'm afraid it's hardly a valid point to make to your shareholders. They have been offered a cash option so the future of Chapmans within Universal cannot be used as a defence argument. That will be Universal's problem and any shareholder who agrees with you can take the cash."

Richard looks stunned but says nothing. That exchange can't have done him much good in the eyes of his fellow directors and he knows it.

"Tell me more about the defence options, Mr Benetto," says Miles. "Are you talking about some kind of poison pill strategy?"

Yet again I hear a phrase which, though vaguely familiar, convinces me that I need to know a lot more about acquisitions if I am to play a useful part in forthcoming events and protect my credibility. I'm just grateful that the questions are coming to Benetto and not to me. I try to assume a look of confidence and understanding as we wait for Benetto's reply.

"Don't answer that question mister," says George sharply, looking at his son with exaggerated effect. "I'm not allowing our company's money to be paid to any goddamned lawyers to stop the shareholders getting full value. We either defend this bid fairly or not at all."

The authority and presence which George creates in the room is amazing for such a small, wiry man. He must be over seventy, grey and lined but the voice is still powerful and seems to rule out any argument. Benetto takes the opportunity of moving on and finishing his presentation. He ends with a tactful reminder of the Board's duty to all its shareholders, particularly where there is a large family holding. He recommends that the Board consult the major external shareholders before making their final recommendation – nothing could be worse than Directors who are seen to be acting against the interests of the owners of the business.

Benetto is impressive. Few could get away with such a reminder to this kind of group without sounding insulting or patronising. I should enjoy working with him.

The meeting breaks up with an agreement to meet in 48 hours, after consultations with major shareholders have taken place, we've taken legal advice and everyone has had a chance to think things over. This also ties in with the deadline which Universal set for us to reply to their offer.

I see Benetto out and agree to meet him the following morning at his New York office with Richard. The Board agreed that we should work with Benetto to get in touch with the major shareholders as soon as possible. As I go back to my office, Richard's waiting for me.

"Sorry pal," says Richard, "but I won't be there in the morning. I've told Miles that I'm resigning as President. I don't need all this shit. The headhunters are always contacting me and I know at least two companies who want someone to run their food operations. That's what I'm good at Phil, that's what I love doing. If you'd got any sense you'd come with me."

I'm taken aback by the suddenness and apparent finality of his decision and his manner leaves no room for argument. Half of me says I should join him but the other half feels a certain excitement at the challenge ahead. The adrenalin is beginning to flow at the thought of being in the middle of a substantial takeover battle and I'm excited at the prospect of such new experiences, whatever risks are involved. And I hope that they might make me Acting President though I guess they're more likely to give it to Miles on a temporary basis.

After Richard leaves with a promise to see me for a handover the day after tomorrow, I begin to think seriously about the task ahead. How can I play an active part when I know so little of the financial measures, the words the experts use and the various options open to a company defending a takeover bid. I remember back to my days at Lawrensons which was part of Universal's UK operations. I remember that I knew nothing of management accounting and how it could be used to run a business more effectively. I remember how a young lady called Christine revitalised my career by showing me that financial concepts weren't as complicated as I'd feared. I remember how she left for the States just before me, at the same time as I made the decision to try to get Jean and my children back.

We kept in touch for a while and she came to visit us several times – the children grew quite fond of her. But Jean asked me not to invite her again and I knew why. She suspected that underneath all the social chit-chat, I cared for Chris and she cared for me. And she was probably right though I had hoped that we could stay friends without jeopardising my marriage again.

Yet now I need Chris like never before – in the same way as I needed her at Lawrensons. To explain the words and the concepts in a way which no-one else could ever do for me. And I'll have no trouble in keeping the relationship platonic this time – I've been through that stage and she's probably married by now anyway. It must be two years since I've seen her.

As I get out my telephone book, I know deep down that I'm making a fateful decision but I press the buttons without hesitation.

Chapter 4

The phone's busy. I have butterflies in my stomach, something which doesn't often happen to me these days. I feel slightly relieved that it's engaged but still determined to try again – perhaps reflecting the mixed-up feelings I've always had about Chris. But it's been two years, she might have moved, be engaged, even married. Which of course wouldn't matter because I only want her to help me out during the acquisition. Any ideas of getting together with her went when I decided to go back to Jean. I'm trying hard to convince myself of this but I know deep down that I was only too pleased to find a reason to contact her again.

I try the phone again. Still busy. I look at my watch and see that it's gone 9.30pm. I try phoning Jean but she's engaged too. While I'm waiting I think about Richard and wonder if he's been too impulsive. For a Company President to resign on the day after a takeover bid is unprecedented as far as I know and I wonder what the press will make of it. Will it help or harm Universal's case I wonder?

But when I remember Richard's motivations and his qualities, I realise that he has got it right. I'm sure the Board will accuse him of disloyalty but he's given them a lot of commitment these last four years and successfully transformed their business.

But he just couldn't see any favourable outcome once Universal's bid had come in. If we fight off the bid, we're likely to go to someone else, now or later. Once you're 'in play', as Benetto expressed it, there's no escape. And Richard just wants to get on with running a business, a food business, that's what he loves. He'll probably go on running from one company to another, looking for the freedom that just isn't there inside major businesses these days. He really ought to start his own company, I think to myself.

I pick up the phone again and wonder whom I should call first. I decide to call Jean because that will be a quick call though I know she'll be worried, maybe even annoyed. This time it rings and I hear her familiar warm tones.

"Hi love," I say and I'm pleased when she says "Hi" back in her usual friendly way. "Sorry I haven't called before but it's been quite a day. I've just got one more call to make then I'll be on my way." I decide it's best not to tell Jean who I'm going to call because I know she wouldn't be pleased to hear it.

"OK darling. We've been hearing all about the bid for Chapmans on the TV – it's quite exciting. They seem very anti-British, is that a problem for you?"

"That's the least of my problems love. They know I'm on Chapmans' side. But I've got lots to tell you when I get home – like Richard's resigned for instance."

I hear her catching her breath. "Oh darling, that's awful. I'd better ring Barbara."

"I'd leave it till tomorrow love. They'll want to be on their own tonight, I'm sure."

"You're right. I'll wait up until you come in. Take care and drive safely."

I say goodbye and put the phone down. I think how lucky I am to have a wife who loves me and was willing to give me a second chance after I allowed my obsession with work to drive us apart. Yet still I have no hesitation when I try Chris's number again. Whatever the risks I know I need her to help me while the Universal bid is facing Chapmans.

This time the phone rings and a man's voice says "Hello." I feel a totally unjustified sense of resentment, perhaps remembering how Chris had been hurt by men before I met her.

"Hello," I say, "could I speak to Chris Goodhart please?", feeling nervous, as if an awful lot hangs on the reply.

"Sure," he says, "who shall I say's calling?"

"Philip Moorley."

The phone makes a noise as it's put down and it seems an age before I hear footsteps coming towards it.

"Phil!" says that familiar voice, "it's great to hear from you. How are things?" The American accent has become very strong these last two years and it reminds me how much she might have changed.

"I'm fine Chris, at least I was until today. Have you heard the news about Chapmans?"

"Sure, I thought of you. Did you know I'm with McKenzies now?" McKenzies are recognised as one of the leading management consultants in the world and I know that they take only the best MBAs. She must have moved on from her first job after she left Harvard – that was with a major investment bank based in Wall Street.

"No, I didn't Chris. Well done. Are you enjoying it?"

"Phil, I'm sorry but it's a bit difficult to chat now. I'm just off to a party. Can you call again or maybe arrange to meet?"

My heart leaps as she says this. I want to ask who the man is – a fiance, husband, lover, friend – if only I could behave sensibly and rationally where she is concerned.

"Yes, Chris, of course. But it's extremely urgent. I need some help with the Universal bid. Richard – you remember my boss – has resigned and to be honest I'm out of my depth. Can we meet for a drink to discuss it?"

She's silent for a few seconds. "I guess so Phil. Are you asking me professionally or informally because I could help you either way. I mean it could be a project for McKenzies."

This takes me back a bit – I hadn't thought of paying for advice and I know McKenzies' fees are outrageous. "I haven't got that far Chris. Can we just meet tomorrow evening and talk it through?"

We agree to meet at a bar we both know in Greenwich

Village the next evening – I know I'm going to be in Benetto's office in New York all day.

I put down the phone and think about our conversation. Not quite what I had in mind. I was thinking of the cosy tutorial sessions we used to have in the evenings at Lawrensons, not some formalised, consultancy assignment with the clock ticking away and costing a fortune. This could be the most expensive lesson in history for a man who can't forget an old flame, I think to myself as I clear my desk.

I drive home along the Expressway, failing to keep below the speed limit as usual and, after I leave to make for our suburb, the traffic's so light that I make very good time. I see our executive-style house looking splendid under its own floodlights as I sweep into the drive. I think how lucky I am to be over here, to have a job and a lifestyle which makes my time in Britain seem very mundane and boring by comparison. I could lose it all if Universal take us over. It won't be easy finding a job over here if they boot me out, and they probably will.

Jean's sitting on the sofa in her dressing gown, looking homely and sensuous at the same time, something which only she can do in her very special way. As she smiles at me, I wonder what she'd say if she knew I'd contacted Chris and I hate myself for deceiving her. But I know I'm not going to tell her now.

"Come and tell me all about it love," she says as she switches off the TV and hands me a martini. Suddenly things don't seem quite so bad any more.

Chapter 5

I'm sitting at this bar in Greenwich Village, gazing across the semi-circle to another guy who's also waiting on his own. I can never understand why the Americans have their bars designed this way. The man at the other side is too far away to have a decent conversation and there's none of the feeling of closeness you get in a British pub.

She's fifteen minutes late and I think that maybe she won't come after all. But then I remember how reliable she always was and guess that she must have been delayed by traffic, not uncommon in New York. I order a second Martini (the US version which is one American habit I've really taken to) and think back over an exhausting but exhilarating day. I watched with admiration how a professional like Benetto operates and I find that already I've learned an amazing amount. But I also know how much I still have to learn which makes my meeting with Chris all the more vital. Much as I like Paul Benetto, I couldn't admit to him that I didn't know what he was talking about half the time. Or admit to Fund Managers who are our major shareholders that their Acting President doesn't know what a 'prospective P/E' or a 'Price to book ratio' really are. I can only get so far on my powers of bluff.

Yes Acting President! It's felt good ever since Miles phoned me just before midnight last night. He'll never know what Jean and I were doing at the time, I'm pleased to say. Jean wouldn't stop giggling as I sat on the bed, completely naked, trying to keep a straight face while I accepted the biggest job of my life. Then we went down to celebrate with a drink before going back upstairs to finish what we'd started. It was pretty good, I think to myself, for a couple who've just celebrated their Silver Wedding, even if the 25 years was interrupted by a divorce and four years apart.

I see the fellow opposite look to his right and his eyes widen. I look to my left as she comes in the door. Not at all the Chris I last saw two years ago. More mature, more feminine, no longer the perfectly kept blonde hair; now the curly, tousled look which seems to give her the instant sex appeal she never had before. She literally takes my breath away as she comes over to me and offers her cheek as she might to an old family friend. I oblige with a platonic kiss and she sits down beside me.

I find it hard to keep my eyes off her. She's everything she was when I last saw her and some of the things she wasn't too. She's now got that special something that was missing before. I know that I shouldn't have rung her because something tells me my life will never be quite the same again.

I buy her a drink – she has a mineral water – and ask her to tell me what she's been doing these last two years. I hope she'll tell me what I'm dying to know – whether there's a man in her life. I look to her wedding ring finger but she keeps it infuriatingly out of view. But she knows what I'm thinking – she could usually read my mind.

"Don't worry Phil, I'm not married, not even engaged. I have a number of guys who date me and you spoke to one last night. Okay?"

"Okay," I reply and continue, lying through my teeth, "it was only curiosity. I don't know how someone like you can be in the States for four years without some guy snapping you up. It shows the Americans have no taste or no gumption."

"Maybe I don't want to be tied down. Hadn't you thought of that? Or were you thinking that I was waiting for you?" she says, with laughter showing in her eyes.

"No Chris, you know I'm happily married now," I say, hoping she'll not be convinced, "and that's not the reason I called you, honestly it's not. Anyway, tell me how you got into McKenzies."

She tells me what's happened since I last saw her two years ago. Then she had just left Harvard for her first job in Wall Street. Apparently she couldn't stand working there, the rat race, the bitchiness of the battle for success and recognition. She worked in the Corporate Finance Department of one of the top three investment banks and did a lot of work on acquisitions. But though it was exciting, it was also frustrating – her bosses seemed to want to maximise their fees rather than get the best for their clients and the consultants like Chris were expected to do analyses which achieved this objective rather than give a true picture. She also found the peaks and troughs hard to cope with – very little to do for a while, followed by weeks of hectic burning of midnight oil when a major bid took place.

So it was a relief when a headhunter approached her for an interview with McKenzies. She'd been chosen largely on the strength of her good MBA grade but McKenzies also valued her UK experience and financial background. She loved consulting from the moment she joined – I asked her why.

"Well I guess it's because I like helping people Phil. Often consultancy's about getting people to see their own companies in a true light and I like that process. Remember how I used to enjoy helping you to learn about the financials at Lawrensons. It's the same thing – helping people to see the really important factors in their business."

"And I thought our evening tutorials were more than that," I say, with laughter in my eyes this time. We exchange smiles but neither of us knows what to say next and there's an awkward silence.

Chris breaks it by saying, "OK then Phil, tell me your position at Chapmans and what kind of help you need."

I tell her what's happened so far and she shows me that she knows a lot about these things by her occasional comments and questions. She also shows that she's been reading the press reports but she was staggered to hear about Richard's resignation.

"That's something I've never heard of before Phil – at least not at this stage. It's great for you but not too good for Chapmans' reputation, particularly if you want to stay independent."

I can see that she's right and it's yet more evidence of what Paul Benetto has been telling me all day – that probably the only way of escaping Universal's clutches is for a White Knight to come along. The Fund Managers whom we managed to contact were of the same view as Paul – that the best immediate tactic is to reject the bid as inadequate, then to wait for Universal to come back with more or for someone else to approach us.

I had lunch with Paul's two partners, also very impressive guys, and a selection of Wall Street experts – analysts, stockbrokers, consultants – and they all confirmed one certain fact. Universal want to win this one very badly and they have deliberately placed the first bid so that they can go higher if necessary. Several names were put forward as possible White Knights and two seemed to be favourite – ABT, a tobacco company now diversifying into food, and Royston, a conglomerate and long standing rival of Universal operating in many of the same markets. The general view was that we need not approach anyone for the time being, they will probably come to us, particularly as the word that Chapmans would not mind a White Knight is likely to get around Wall Street.

As I recount this to Chris, she says, "Yes, I guess Benetto will make sure the rumour gets around – he's a sharp cookie. But I'm not sure what is behind it from Chapmans' point of view. Is it to drive the bid price up or is it to fight off Universal at all costs?"

"It's both Chris. There's a lot of anti-British feeling, which makes my position particularly interesting, but there's also concern about Universal's reputation for closing down operations and cutting jobs. We feel that it's less likely with another acquirer – or at least it could be. Anyway, it's in the shareholders' interests to drive the price up to the highest level and a bit of competition's bound to help."

"Yes I see. What a beautiful situation. I quite envy you – who'd have thought you'd be involved in something like this when you were at Lawrensons? You were terrified of Universal and all their financial information demands I remember. Until you realised how straightforward it really was."

"Until you helped me to see that Chris and that's what I want you to do again for me. Richard's gone, I haven't got a Chief Financial Officer and Carl Palinski, my Controller, is just as much out of his depth as me. And, rightly or wrongly, people expect a President, even an Acting President ..."

"You're President Phil! You didn't tell me that before. That's wonderful – congratulations." She gives me a lovely sincere smile and I see again how she's changed, how she's matured, how she's become so absolutely stunning. I think that if I couldn't help falling for her four years ago, what chance do I have now? What have I started?

"Thanks," I reply. "I must admit I was surprised. Though from one or two things I heard from Benetto today, my British credentials may have been important. The Chapmans are no fools and I expect Miles Chapman to keep a very close watch on things. He's been on the phone to me several times today."

There's a silence and she breaks it by saying, "Phil, I mentioned over the phone that there's this problem with McKenzies. We aren't supposed to do any work outside our contract and in any case I have very little spare time. Is there any chance that I could help in an open way, as your advisor?"

I think about this – it's not really what I had in mind. But I see her point – a private arrangement would put her in a difficult position with her employer and that's the last thing I want to do. And how would the private sessions seem to others at Chapmans? We would probably have to meet in another location and the travelling wouldn't be easy. And I guess I'd have to start lying to Jean again. No, the more I think about it, the more I can see she's right.

After all, I am now Acting President and my spending limits are pretty high. And having heard about Benetto's enormous fees this morning, a little more isn't going to make too much difference. Yes, I'll appoint her as my official advisor – the only thing I need to do is to convince Miles and he's not likely to turn me down. He needs me more than I need him, since Richard's resignation.

"OK Chris, you're on," I say, "what's your daily rate?"

"$1500 a day Phil – that's the junior consultant rate, would you believe."

"Well, let's just have a couple of sessions and see how it goes. But I need help now or it's no good. Can you give me any time tomorrow?"

"Sure, I've already freed my diary."

She's an even sharper operator than she used to be. She sees me as a business opportunity and probably nothing more. She confirms this by saying, "Phil, there is one condition as far as I'm concerned." This has a familiar ring and I know what's coming.

"Yes?" I ask unnecessarily.

"There must be no romantic strings attached. I know I cared for you once but that was before you got together with Jean again. And I liked your kids very much – how are they by the way?"

For the next fifteen minutes we chat away like old friends and I bring her up to date on my children and their various accomplishments in the US education system. She asks about Jean – they always got on very well – and we agree that it would be nice for her to come and see us again. I know that Jean won't be happy about that but I say nothing.

As I order another drink, she tells me that she must be off in a few minutes and we fix for her to come to Chapmans at 10.30 am the following day.

"Tell me the sort of things you want to cover Phil"

"Well, it's the arithmetic of takeover bids really Chris. P/E Ratios and the various types – historic, prospective, exit. Also the relevance of asset values to the bid price. And Benetto has been talking a lot about goodwill and brand valuations. Something about the UK and US accounting conventions being different or something."

"Right, that's no problem. I'm fairly well clued up on

those things. There's nothing really complex about P/E
Ratios – you understand the principles surely?"

"Yes, I guess so. I know that the E is for Earnings
which is profits after tax."

"Right," she nods in confirmation.

"And that Earnings Per Share is the Earnings divided by
all the shares issued."

"Right, so it's the share of profits which every
shareholder is entitled to. But remember it's not
necessarily all paid in dividend – some will be retained and
ploughed back into the business."

I can already see that mission to explain, which is so
strong in her, shining in her eyes. I can tell that she really
enjoys doing this, whatever her feelings for me. I guess that
she's also attracted to the idea of helping someone involved
in such a high profile takeover battle at this early stage in
her career.

"OK," I say, "so the P/E Ratio is the price of the share
in the market divided by the earnings per share. I
understand that but I'm not so sure of its meaning to Wall
Street or its relevance to acquisitions. And, as I
mentioned, there seem to be several versions of it."

"It's no good Phil," she says, "I need some numbers to
show you, I need a flipchart, we can't do it here."

"No, of course, Chris. I remember you were always
lost without your flipchart."

We both smile at this reminder of our times together at
Lawrensons and our eyes meet for a second. But we both
look away quickly, as if we're now afraid to go back to the
closeness we used to share.

As we walk out of the bar together into the daylight a
few minutes later, I'm struck once again by her beauty.
What absurd vanity makes me think she would want to take
up with me? Maybe a few years ago but not now. In any
case, I have Jean and the kids at home. It would be crazy
to throw all that away again. But I still look forward to
seeing her tomorrow with a special kind of excitement
which nothing else can match. Not even the thought of
being Acting President of Chapmans and the prospect of
fighting off the Universal bid.

Chapter 6

The next morning I'm in early before 8 o'clock and there's a handwritten note from Richard on my desk.

"I'd like to see you urgently. Please pop in."

I remember that I'm seeing him today for a handover and wonder if this will be his last day at Chapmans. I also remember that Miles wants to see me about releasing the news of Richard's resignation to the press but I guess he won't be in till 9 o'clock, he never is.

I walk down the corridor to Richard's office and find him clearing out files and putting them into a box. I will be moving into his office soon but I'm not sure what I'll do about a secretary – take over Karen or keep Tracy. That will be difficult, I think to myself but such a detail soon fades from my mind as Richard hits me with yet another bombshell. I thought I'd had enough shocks this week but this beats all.

"Phil, you ought to know. Barbara and I have split up."

"Oh Richard, I'm so sorry," I reply and can't think of anything else to say except rather irrelevantly. "When did it happen?"

"Last night. She's kicked me out old buddy. She says she's had enough of the way I make impulsive decisions without consulting her. But it's not really that sudden. She didn't want to leave Britain, she and the kids loved it over there and she's blamed me ever since. My leaving Chapmans without consulting her and facing the prospect

of another move was just too much for her. I suppose I
deserve it."

I feel sorry for both of them because I can see both
points of view. And I also realise how little you really know
about what goes on behind closed doors, even with people
you think you know well.

"Richard," I say, "do you mind if I ring Jean – she and
Barbara are so close. I'm sure she'd want to know."

"No need pal, Barbara's ringing her this morning. And
we both want you two guys to stay as our friends, whatever
happens."

The phone rings and Richard answers.

"Hi Miles," he says, "Yes, he's here. Sure I will."

I look at my watch. Miles in at 8 o'clock! Times really
have changed. Richard tells me that Miles wants a
debriefing from yesterday and I agree to go up right away.
Before I leave I ask Richard, "When are you finishing
Richard? We need to meet some time today."

"We're announcing it to the staff about lunchtime, the
same time as we release it to the Press, and I'll finish
tonight. Can we meet mid afternoon?"

"Do you have to go Richard?" I say, though without
much hope. "Surely it's not too late. You could go on
running the business and let Miles and me look after the
Universal bid."

"It's too late for that Phil. Miles and his father wouldn't
let me change my mind anyway. I've really hurt them, like
I seem to have hurt everybody else. And there's no way
we're going to get out of this one. Universal mean to have
us and in my view the Chapmans have accepted that
they're going to have to sell. They're just trying to get the
best price from Universal or this White Knight they keep
talking about. Who do you think that will be?"

"Royston or ABT are the current bets in Wall Street."

"Well I'd prefer either to Universal but I've had enough
of working for big corporations. That's what I can't make
Barbara understand." He looks at me rather pathetically
and I find it hard to believe that this is the same man who's
driven me so hard and taught me so much these last four
years. "And there's another reason why Miles and George

want me to go Phil," he says.

"What's that?"

"They want you as President. Miles rates you highly, particularly compared with me now that I've let them down. And they seem to think that having a President from the UK prevents them being accused of Anti-British feeling. It's a funny old world."

I remember that Miles is waiting for me upstairs and I leave Richard looking forlornly at the company mission statement which he has always kept so proudly on his wall – 'To make Chapmans the top name in quality, added value food products throughout the USA,' it begins. He hardly seems to notice as I open his office door and take the lift to the Board Room.

As I go up in the lift (I can never get used to calling it the elevator), I think about what Richard said and how it confirms the strength of my position. But does Miles rate me that much or does he just need me in the present crisis? I know I've always suffered from lack of confidence but can he really believe that I know enough to be an effective President during the battle that's to come? On the other hand, do I know any less than the average President in this situation, unless they happen to come from a financial background? Anyway I should now be in a strong position when I press to have Chris as my advisor.

The meeting with Miles is very successful. We seem to be getting on really well since Richard resigned. He asks me to relay all that happened the previous day and I update him fully. We agree the text of the press release and he asks me to inform Benetto and synchronise it with the staff announcement. I'm pleased that the conversation doesn't get round to the financial technicalities and after about 45 minutes, he gets up and says, "I have to see my father Phil – anything else urgent? I'll be back about midday."

"Yes Miles, just one thing. I feel that I need someone else, apart from Benetto, as a personal advisor. To help me with the technicalities and to provide some kind of check on the guy. I know he's good but we are putting an awful lot of trust in him."

"Who do you have in mind?"

"Someone from McKenzies. She used to be my Accountant in the UK with Universal. She did a Harvard MBA and she's worked in Wall Street. More important I can work with her. Miles, as I've told you before, I'm not really a financial man and a lot of this is new to me."

Miles narrows his eyes, leans forward and says, "Attractive is she Phil?" and then smiles. "Of course you can hire her – you're the President now and I'll judge you by results. If we can afford Benetto's fees, we can afford McKenzies'. But don't mix business with pleasure old pal. Richard told me about you and Jean when you were back in the UK. I'd hate to see my new President's marriage breaking up too. I suppose you've heard about Richard and Barbara?"

He's now picked up his briefcase and is walking out the office so I don't get much chance to reply. I rather resent his implication but remember the old-fashioned attitudes some of these Americans have, particularly families with a strong religious tradition like the Chapmans.

I return to my office and Tracy brings me up to date with my messages. Again, I seem to be in a strange sort of vacuum with very little to do – all the daily routine's been taken away from me since the Universal bid. And there isn't too much I have to do about the bid either – Benetto's the sort of man who takes things out of your hands. All very well if he's good and I can check on what he's doing – hence the importance of Chris's contribution.

She arrives ten minutes early and I ask Tracy to fetch her from reception. I tidy my thinning head of hair in the mirror in my office and check that my favourite patterned tie, chosen specially this morning, is straightened. I feel like I once did at Lawrensons – like a schoolboy on his first date – and I laugh to myself at my own vanity.

She walks in behind Tracy and this time she offers her hand to shake in a very businesslike way. I see Tracy giving her a rather pointed sideways look, the sort that one attractive girl often gives to another. And I am curious to know what Tracy's thinking – she seemed a little surprised when I mentioned this last minute entry in my diary earlier on, even though I tried to make my voice sound as matter of fact as possible.

"Oh, I see you've got a flipchart – good," she says as she walks in and sits on the chair opposite my desk.

"I always have one in here Chris – you persuaded me of its advantages years ago. How about a coffee before we start?"

While we drink our coffee, I fill her in with more detail on my day with Benetto. I see she's got a copy of Chapmans' Annual Report with her.

"OK Phil, let's go over the financial position. It'll confirm my understanding and make sure we're on the same wavelength."

"Right. The bid price per share is $51."

"Fine. Now let's check the number of shares issued in the Annual Report. They're all ordinary, no preference shares, am I right?"

"I'm sure you've told me before but it was a long time ago. Just remind me what preference shares are."

"They are special shares which have first claim on dividend but only up to a fixed percentage. They're fairly unusual these days and they aren't usually included when analysts calculate shareholder measures."

"What sort of measures do you mean – the P/E Ratio?"

"Yes that's one, but I'll come back to them shortly. Now, let's see how many ordinary shares Chapman has on issue – they often call them common stock over here. Can I take the figure from the Annual Report? You haven't issued any since then have you?"

"No. We issued some new shares two years ago but none since. The number of ordinary shares issued is 9.804 million and the par value is $5. Par is the US phrase for nominal value, am I right?"

"Yes and what was the market price before the bid?"

"$40 or thereabouts."

"Right. So we can calculate the market capitalisation. Do you know what that means?"

I decide I'd better remind her that things are rather different from the days back at Lawrensons when I knew very little about these matters.

"Chris. You can assume a lot more knowledge than you

did before. I have remembered and used most of what you explained then. Also I had to work out the bid for Richard and Miles, our Chairman when it first came in. I calculated about $500 million which ties in with what the press are now quoting."

"OK Phil. I'm sorry. I'll speed up and you slow me down if I go too fast. But the market capitalisation calculation is fundamental to the relevance of P/E Ratios in an acquisition. Let's put up the pre and post bid figures."

She moves to the flipchart and I remember that look in her eyes when she gets into her teaching role. She's obviously a born teacher and I wonder if she ought to move into some kind of training career – with her looks and personality, she could be phenomenally successful, even if trainees might have problems keeping their mind on the subject. I have trouble myself as she walks across to my desk to pick up a marker pen and I see her slender legs with the skirt of her coordinated outfit cut well above the knee, something she would never have worn when she was back in the UK.

She writes on the flipchart:

TOTAL SHARES ISSUED		MARKET PRICE PRE-BID		PRE-BID MARKET CAPITALISATION
9.804m	x	$40	=	$392.16m
PRICE		BID		VALUE
9.804m	x	$51	=	$500.004m

"Hmm. I guess they planned it just to exceed the 500 million mark," says Chris, "so that they can get the right headlines. Universal's PR always was clever. What's the percentage premium over pre-bid price?"

I'm stuck for a minute, my old fear of financial matters getting in the way of common sense. Then I think – premium? That's what Benetto mentioned yesterday. The excess of the bid price of 51 over the previous level of 40. I'm just going to calculate that when Chris says, "Twenty-seven point five per cent. Did you get that – 500.004 divided by 392.16?"

"I did it by taking 51 and dividing by 40 but it's obviously the same ratio. Which way is it normally done?"

"Could be either. The brokers usually think per share but those into serious analysis will obviously need to look at total value, partly because they also need to relate it to assets on the Balance Sheet. We'll have a look at that shortly. Now let's calculate the P/Es. What were your earnings after tax in the last year's published accounts?"

I turn to the published accounts and find the Profit & Loss Account. I never fail to be confused by the American terminology which calls the P & L – 'Income Statement'. Just as I'd got used to UK terminology I had to learn a whole new set of words in the States. The Profit & Loss Account looks like this:

	$000
Sales Turnover	678,274
Cost of Sales	382,747
Gross Profit	295,527
Operating Expenses	229,201
Earnings from Operations	66,326
Interest Expense	15,281
Earnings before Tax	51,045
Taxes	18,840
Net Earnings	32,205

I call out, "32,205 thousand dollars or 32.205 million. Do you need to know dividend?"

"No," she says, "dividends aren't really directly relevant to acquisition valuations though they do affect other market indicators. I'll cover that another time. Now let's have a look at the pre and post bid P/Es."

She writes:

	PER SHARE		TOTAL	
	PRE-BID	BID	PRE BID	BID
PRICE	40	51	392.160	500.004
EARNINGS	3.28	3.28	32.205	32.205
PRICE/EARNINGS RATIO	12.2	15.5	12.2	15.5

"So you see how you can calculate P/Es either way. Per share, which is the way the market talks about share ratings on a day to day basis. Or in total which is how acquisitions are valued. Are you happy with these figures?"

I check carefully because I know how vital it is for me to understand this thoroughly. I see that the Earnings Per Share of $3.28 is actually quoted in the Annual Report but I also double check its calculation – 32.205 divided by 9.804 shares issued. I now feel ready to move forward.

"Right Chris, now can you tell me exactly what the P/E ratio means in normal times and also during an acquisition? And what is meant by historic, prospective and exit P/Es? And I see from the Wall Street Journal this morning that our price has gone up to $56, which will presumably give us yet another P/E."

"Yes, that means that the market believes Universal are going to have to pay more. Mr Benetto's no doubt been doing his stuff for you – spreading the word. It builds up shareholder expectations nicely and makes it much less likely that they'll accept $51. Anyway, one thing at a time. Let's concentrate on what the P/E means first."

I sit back and listen, completely bowled over by the range of her knowledge and the way she puts it over. And, of course, her stunning appearance, which I try to put out of my mind for the time being because I really need to understand all this if I am to be a credible Company President during the next few weeks.

"Remember that Earnings per share and Price per share cannot easily be compared between one company and

another," she says. "Each company has a different financial
structure because of the particular history of funding that
business. OK?"

I nod in agreement and comment, "Right, but they do
compare the relative *growth* in price and earnings don't
they? That's been our problem since we issued our new
shares. Our earnings increased but, with the new shares,
our earnings *per share* declined the year after. Earnings per
share dilution am I right?"

"Right. My, you have moved on since the old days in
the UK. Those evenings we spent together obviously paid
off."

I think to myself that they didn't pay off in the way I
wanted them to at the time but decide I'd better not say so.
I must also decide how I'm going to tell Jean about Chris
being back on the scene. Now that she's here at Chapmans
openly, I can't risk it leaking out and Jean finding that I've
been keeping it from her. I put this painful thought out of
my mind as she goes on to explain the relevance of the
various P/E measures.

"So, you can't really compare Price and Earnings figures
separately but you can compare their relationship with each
other. That's what the P/E is, the number of times that the
price is the multiple of the last full year's published
earnings."

"So it can be quite out of date then. I mean the profits
can be nearly a year old. In our case, it's May now so it's
five months since our last year end."

"Right. That's where the prospective P/E comes in – I'll
come back to that quite soon. But are you happy about the
concept? At the share price before Universal put in their
bid, the shares were trading at just over twelve times
earnings."

"In other words, buyers were having to pay the
equivalent of twelve year's profits to buy the shares."

"Yes, that's right."

"But how does that compare with the average?"

"In the US the average is now about 14. In the UK the
Stock Market's declined recently and I think it was about
11 last time I heard."

"OK Chris, now let me get this right. The US average is 14 but Chapmans was 12 so the future prospects of Chapmans were less than the average US company."

"Yes, or at least that was the perception of the market. The excess of price over earnings really reflects the confidence which people buying the shares are showing in relation to the most recently published profits. It's how the future prospects relate to the recent past and that must depend on buyers' perceptions. They pay the price they do for shares because of their expectations of future improvement."

I think about this, and how simple this concept really is. The number of years' profits you're buying at today's market price. But then I remember something that was mentioned at the Board Meeting the evening of the day the bid came in.

"But how does this relate to the yield Chris? They talk of yield in the Stock Market don't they? And one of our Directors mentioned the implications for Universal's yield if they pay a high P/E to acquire us."

"The yield usually quoted in Stock Markets is the dividend yield which I mentioned earlier. I guess he would just be thinking of the yield on investment for Universal if they pay the price they're offering. That's just another way of thinking about the P/E. Let me show you."

She writes up:

$$\frac{PRICE}{EARNINGS} = \frac{51}{3.28} = 15.5 \quad \frac{EARNINGS}{PRICE} \quad \frac{3.28}{51} = 6.4\% \text{ Yield}$$

Again I see just how simple these things are once you break through the jargon. The yield is just the reverse of the P/E. The Director was merely saying that the higher the price they pay the lower the return to them will be.

"So the higher the price and the P/E, the lower the return you will get if you buy those shares," I confirm rather obviously, keen to demonstrate my new understanding to Chris.

"In a Stock Exchange context that depends on dividend and future capital growth of the shares. Those who play

the market often look for shares with what they regard as
an undervalued P/E. But in Universal's case you're right.
If Universal go to a P/E of 20 to get Chapmans, which the
gossip on Wall Street says they might, they will only be
getting a 5% return. But that assumes last year's earnings
as the only return. They may well have plans to sell off
assets and make savings on their US operations by merging
Chapmans with their other companies. So they'll be
preparing their own internal cash flow estimates and doing
a DCF calculation – remember that from Lawrensons?"

"Yes, we use it a lot here for our investment decisions,"
I reply truthfully, rather pleased with myself because I was
the one who introduced it to Chapmans.

Chris continues, "And they will also have a model which
calculates the impact of the bid on their Earnings per Share
which will be quite a complex calculation, particularly as
they have offered cash and share alternatives."

"OK Chris," I reply, "I'm quite happy with the level of
complexity at present. We can cover that another day.
And isn't there some issue about accounting conventions
too – writing off goodwill?"

"Yes. We'll leave that till later too. Let me just finish
off by covering the labels they give the P/E – Historic, Exit,
Prospective. They're all quite easy really."

I think to myself that it's only easy once you get used to
the words, have someone like Chris to explain them and
then be given time to absorb it all. I sit expectantly,
waiting for her to fill the remaining gaps in my knowledge
of P/E Ratios.

"Right. We've almost covered them actually, except
that we didn't use those labels."

She's standing by the flipchart, so full of enthusiasm, so
desperately wanting me to understand, that I have no
problem holding my concentration, despite the other things
on my mind – the news about Richard and Barbara, the
thought of meeting Richard to say goodbye and take things
over from him, the Board Meeting this evening and the
difficult weeks ahead. Such is the magnetism of her
personality and her desire to make me understand.

"OK," she continues. "Historic P/E is the one based on

last year's profits, the figure we calculated of 12.2. That's the one which you see in the FT and the Wall Street Journal."

"But Universal bid 15 times earnings so what do we call that?"

"The Exit P/E, or at least the one they are proposing at present. The Exit P/E is the one which is finally agreed for the takeover price so it will only be the Exit P/E if our shareholders accept the bid at $51 which we now know is very unlikely."

"Fine – what about the Prospective P/E? Where does that fit in?"

"That's based on the forecast of earnings for the next full year's results. Have you given any indication to the analysts of what your results will be?"

"No, Miles and his father don't like us talking to the Wall Street crowd. The Chapmans have always kept their cards very close to their chest."

"Maybe that's why your P/E is lower than average," says Chris, looking concerned. "You just have to talk to them these days Phil because, if you don't, they'll make their own assumptions. I checked with some analysts at my old firm and they're assuming $35 million. Is that about right?"

One thing I always have at my fingertips is the latest estimate profit for the year which Universal always wanted to know and which Chris encouraged me to monitor when we were both at Lawrensons. I know that the 35 million is about right and I tell her so.

"OK, so per share that's 35 million divided by 9.804 shares equals $3.57," she says, punching numbers into her calculator. Then she writes up:

$$\frac{Price}{Earnings} \quad \frac{40}{3.57} = 11.2 \quad \text{(pre-bid)} \qquad \frac{51}{3.57} = 14.3 \quad \text{(bid)}$$

"So the prospective P/E before the bid was 11.2. Really Phil, that was very low for a food company. The average in US food companies is higher than the overall average of 14 so your rating was really low."

"Did it matter that much?" I ask and instantly realise what a stupid question it is. Of course – that was one reason why we were so vulnerable to Universal!

She replies to this effect, giving me that withering look I remember so well.

"Phil. Can't you see that it's the low P/E which has enabled Universal to bid at that level. If the Chapmans had talked to the analysts and convinced them of your future prospects, you would have had more buyers, a higher price and a higher P/E. As it is Universal may get you with a prospective P/E of under 20 which is not bad at all for them. Good food companies don't come cheap, particularly when the market knows that companies like Universal and Nestlé are wanting to expand into the States."

I know how right she is and how the Chapmans, Richard and I have not been fully carrying out our top management role. We've all been too inwardly focused, allowing the Chapman family tradition of secrecy and Richard's desire to get on with running the business to obscure our responsibilities to keep in touch with shareholders and potential investors. And I must share the blame because I should have filled the gap if my responsibilities in respect of the Finance Function had any meaning.

Just as I'm thinking this over, the phone rings and Tracy tells me that Jean is on the line. Without thinking I ask for her to be put through and then feel ridiculously guilty to be talking to Jean while looking at Chris across the other side of the desk.

"Darling," says that warm familiar voice, "I've got Barbara here – has Richard told you?"

"Yes love," I reply, "he told me this morning."

"Well I think Barbara's realised she acted a bit hastily and she wants to see Richard. Is he there?"

"I think so," I say, wondering and fearing what's coming next.

"Well Barbara wants me with her so we're both coming over and she'd like to have lunch with Richard somewhere near the office. I don't suppose you'll be free by any chance? I know things must be pretty hectic."

I look at Chris and a feeling of panic wells up in me. If only I'd told Jean that I was seeing Chris. I start to sweat as I think how to react.

"I'll have to see if Richard's available love. I'm not sure if I can make it. I'll call you back in five minutes."

I put the phone down and look at Chris once again, wishing fervently that I'd resisted the temptation to contact her again but knowing that it was somehow inevitable. There are now two women in my life again and I can't do without either of them.

Chapter 7

Once again I'm in the Board Room and I look down the table to see a row of faces, looking serious and concerned but paying close attention to what's being said. And, believe it or not, it's me they're paying attention to as I'm quickly running through the position prior to handing over to Paul Benetto.

It was Paul's idea that I do this; he said the Board should feel that I am in command of the situation, even if he is coping with the detail. It is fortunate that my morning session with Chris has given me sufficient confidence to make the statement though I'm praying that there'll be no questions or other interruptions. I wonder what the Board would say if they knew that I only learnt about exit P/Es this morning as I confidently declare:

"And the price of $56 in the market today indicates that the analysts are expecting an exit P/E of 17 and we hear that some speculators are still looking for shares to buy, so it could go higher by tomorrow evening."

My heart skips a beat as one of the non-executive Directors asks a question. Is he testing me?

"Shouldn't that P/E be expressed on a prospective rather than historic basis Mr Moorley? Isn't it the forecast earnings we should be thinking about?"

My initial panic suddenly fades for I know the answer, thanks to this morning's work. Nevertheless I turn to Benetto for reassurance as I reply.

"On a prospective basis the initial bid from Universal is just over 14, based on our forecast EPS of $3.57. If the bid price were to be the current market price of $56 this would give us..."

"Nearly 16," says Benetto, "which I have to say is still not too high for a food company of your standing, particularly as we're in a bid situation that is hostile and probably competitive. I still stick to the prediction I made when I last saw you gentlemen. If it gets competitive with one or more other bidders coming in, the exit P/E could go to 20 which would mean $65 or even $70 if you take prospective earnings. Your share price prior to this bid was very poorly rated and the extent of this is now being shown."

I see George Chapman suddenly straighten in his chair.

"I always knew these Wall Street guys under-rated us," he says. "Why do you think that is Mr Benetto?"

How will Paul handle this; I'm certain his view is much the same as the one Chris expressed to me this morning. And I don't think George will like it.

"I can perhaps best quote my own perceptions before I got to know you better. We knew the underlying strengths of your traditional businesses. We were also impressed by the development of the brands and the moves into higher value products during the last two or three years. But no-one has ever told us the underlying strategy behind it all. You were regarded as a mystery company and we never saw the management except at the formal results presentations. The analysts gave up asking for meetings – they've had so many requests rejected. And they tend not to recommend shares of companies they don't fully understand. And there is also one more very important factor which has held the share price down."

I look round the table again and see how Benetto's tactful authority seems to have won them over. Even Miles and George, who might well be defensive about this implied criticism of their investor relations policy, seem to be accepting his points. And so do I. I know only too well that I should have been working with Richard to persuade the Chapmans to open up the communication channels.

Benetto carries on.

"There was always a belief that the Chapman family would reject any takeover bid. We now know that this will not be the case if the bid is right but that perception was bound to cause the share price to be lower than other companies with an unrestricted shareholding."

Benetto, who is sitting next to me, now seems effectively to have taken control of the discussion and I confirm this by telling the Board that he will now cover the more detailed issues. I sit back and relax for a while as he goes over ground which is now very familiar to me – the arguments for rejection of the bid and the near certainty of a second offer from Universal, with or without a competitive bid.

I think back to events earlier in the day. The embarrassment of a meeting between Chris and Jean was just avoided. Richard did not want to see Barbara at Chapmans so they met at a local restaurant. I excused myself, thinking in any case that my presence was hardly going to help. When I saw Richard in the afternoon, he said that nothing had been resolved but that he would be seeing Barbara again this evening. He did not sound optimistic and said that we had better cancel plans for the two families to meet over the coming weekend.

Weekend! I seem to have lost all track of time. It was Tuesday morning when the fax came through and it's now Thursday evening yet it seems as if several years have passed since things were normal. Only on Monday I was hearing an agency presentation about an advertising campaign for a new product launch next quarter. I hope that Jane, my Marketing Manager, has got it all under control.

At least the weekend should give me time to talk to Jean and tell her about Chris's new role. I'm hopeful that she'll understand but there's a nagging doubt in my mind that she'll suspect my motives. There's also a nagging doubt that she'll be right too.

Chris left early afternoon, after we'd continued working through a sandwich lunch and we agreed to have a further session early tomorrow morning to go over some of the accounting issues which are important to acquisitions. Over lunch she defined some more terms for me and covered one more ratio – what the Americans call 'Price to Book', a phrase which has been quoted to me a few times by Benetto.

Like most of these things it's quite simple once you get the idea. It's just the multiple of the price per share to the assets per share and she showed it on the flipchart in the same way as the P/E:

	Per Share ($)	Total ($m)
Price (Universal Bid)	51	500.004
Balance Sheet Book Value	18.36	180.000
Price to Book	2.78	2.78

I remembered the figure of $180m which I'd taken from the Balance Sheet on Tuesday morning when I first discussed the Universal offer with Miles and Richard. It's the net book value of all assets, after taking off all liabilities, both short and long term. Thus it represents the amount which, assuming that balance sheet values are realised, the business would raise if closed down and sold off. Chris mentioned that this is often called 'Net Worth' in the UK.

She also mentioned that part of the $320m difference between the offer and the book value could be under valuation of assets purchased some time ago. But the major reason for such a difference is usually likely to be the intangibles. The brands, the market share, the staff, the management (partly Richard, I thought to myself) and the ability to make future profits. In accounting terms, this difference is 'goodwill' and it is the accounting treatment of this which apparently creates great controversy and is so important to acquisition battles, particularly between US and UK companies. I'll hear more of this tomorrow and whether it's the impact of Chris's personality, my new-found interest in the subject or my desperate need to know, I'm really looking forward to finding out more. If, five years ago, anyone had told me that I'd be interested in the differences between international accounting treatments of goodwill, I'd have laughed at them. How times have changed!

The fact that I'm sitting in the Boardroom of a large US company at 8.45 pm, rather than watching television with Jean and the kids, is another reflection of changing times. I'm hoping that this battle will not go on too long because I know how much Jean needs my support at home and how, once before, my long working hours started us on the road to separation and divorce.

Benetto is continuing his summary of the options but there is no doubt that the outcome of the meeting is now a formality. There is little to lose (very little 'downside' as Benetto calls it) by rejection of the Universal bid. If there is no other bid the share price is likely to stay around the bid level because the market now regards Chapmans as being 'in-play' and a potential future acquisition candidate. In any case the P/E at the bid price is not unreasonable for a well run food business with good future prospects and, though Richard's resignation was a shock to Wall Street, it need not affect the long-term share price if the right investor relations channels are set up.

At this point Benetto turns to me and then to the rest of the Board saying: "And if I may say so gentlemen, I think you have the right man here to give Wall Street the necessary re-assurance. I know that Philip is very aware of his responsibility to communicate with all shareholders and I'm sure you'll give him your backing. Otherwise the share price will only slide back to the $40 mark again."

"But Mr Benetto," says Miles, "surely that's academic isn't it? You've told me and others here several times that Universal will come back again with a higher bid."

"I believe that to be true sir, but you must appreciate that I can't guarantee it. I'm just trying to reassure you that, with the right advice and with good communications with the Street, you should have nothing to lose by rejection anyway."

The meeting now concentrates on the reasons to be given for rejection and it is left to Miles, Benetto and me to draft a reply to Universal and a press release the following day. The Directors suggest a number of additions to the main message that the bid undervalues the company, emphasising in particular its strong brands and future profit potential. They also request that mention be made of the need to protect Chapmans' identity as an independent business and to safeguard the interests of employees. Several Directors want also to mention the need to keep ownership in the US but Benetto is concerned about the way the other shareholders may perceive this. He makes the point that the Investment Fund Managers who hold Chapmans' shares will accept the best for their investors whichever company or country the money comes from. He even has doubts about mentioning the interests of employees and suggests including the words "as far as possible". He is concerned not to close options for potential competitive bidders. I notice how Miles looks at George Chapman who nods his agreement to this caveat – George is still calling the shots in this Boardroom.

It's nearly 11 o'clock before I reach home and, after a long day, I'm looking forward to the comfort of Jean, particularly the prospect of her warm body in bed. I've tried to ring several times but it's been busy every time. As I enter the driveway, I see another car there and realise that it's Barbara's. Despite my sympathy for her and Richard, I can't help feeling irritation too. I walk in and they're both sitting on the sofa. Jean is comforting Barbara whose face is red and blotchy with tears. There's no Martini ready for me this time.

"Darling," says Jean, "how are you? I hope you don't mind but Barbara's staying the night. She and Richard had another terrible row and he's gone. He says he's going to take a job back in England."

Chapter 8

The next morning I'm in even earlier, at 7.30 am, to have an hour with Karen, Richard's secretary, going over outstanding issues which Richard left for me. It is typical of Karen and her commitment to Chapmans, that a request to come in that early did not seem anything unusual – she's been used to working all hours for the various Company Presidents she's served over the years. I've reserved judgement as to who will be my secretary until the bid situation is resolved one way or the other, but have asked Karen and Tracy to cooperate closely together, sharing out work as appropriate.

Chris is due to arrive at 9.30 am so I take the opportunity for a quick briefing from Jane to tell me the outcome of the advertising campaign review and also to update me about other issues. Very little seems to have happened during the three days I've been out of circulation and I have time to question Jane on the way the staff are taking the news. She tells me that Richard's resignation has been the biggest blow and we agree that it would be useful for me to visit as many departments as possible later today to show the flag and tell them what I can. I tell her I'll try if nothing else happens to distract me. She tells me, with a lovely combination of respect and assertiveness, that there should be nothing else more important for a Company President than talking to his employees. I decide I'll reserve all afternoon to do just that.

Jane always was an assertive woman and I feel quite proud that it was I who spotted her working in the market research department. In the four years I've been at Chapmans she's risen through the ranks and overtaken many more qualified product managers who may have MBAs and be more analytical but don't have Jane's motivation to gain market share and beat the competition.

She's an uncomplicated woman with many friends and a wonderfully relaxed approach – her only weakness seems to be her inability to resist Chapmans' and any other food products but her plumpness seems to suit her cheerful, down to earth personality.

Henry Goss, who manages the sales force, is another cheerful extrovert. Henry is popular with everyone and seems to motivate his sales force exceptionally well. His main weakness is a tendency to chase business at all costs, irrespective of the economics of doing so. We often have discussions about this but Henry's enthusiasm usually wins me over.

When I call him in at about 9.15 am, he's got a summary of last week's sales figures and a prepared list of issues to discuss with me. He tells me that both sales representatives and major customers are concerned about the possibility of a Universal acquisition. The representatives have heard rumours of Universal's reputation for rationalising operations following acquisitions and major customers, at least according to Henry, value the independence and flexibility of Chapmans. Apparently Universal's US companies are much less cooperative, particularly with regard to small order deliveries and special customer promotions. Knowing Henry's tendency always to say yes rather than no to customers, I think perhaps Universal have got it right. But now is not the time to say so.

As, a few minutes later, Chris drinks a coffee before we get down to work I mention this issue to her.

"Do you produce reports of major customer profitability in the way I showed you at Lawrensons Phil?" she asks.

"Sure," I say, "every half year. It was the first major management accounting system I put in. But I'm afraid that Henry is not really a numbers man and passes them on to his account managers without looking for the action points. I've been meaning to do something about it."

"Hmm," replies Chris, perhaps remembering the same initial resistance from me and my management staff at Lawrensons, "though reports of major customer profitability won't cope with the problem of small, uneconomic orders and customers. You really need a Pareto analysis for that."

"What's that?" I reply, thinking again how useful it is to have someone like Chris as a sounding board to discuss this kind of issue.

"Pareto analysis is what shows you the 80/20 pattern – how 80% of customers give you 20% of revenue and vice versa. We've not got time today but, when this is all over, maybe I could help you."

"More business for McKenzies?" I say with a smile. "I know you consultants always find a way to sell on and I wouldn't expect you to be any exception Chris."

She smiles back and I feel some of the old warmth between us, largely as a result of our working together again. We've had to rebuild our working relationship and we seem to have done so pretty quickly, after an uncertain start. She asks me about Jean and the children and, for a few minutes, we talk about them but soon we're back to the importance of the 'price to book' ratio which she described yesterday. First of all I ask her what it is called in the UK, also the significance to the market of a high or low figure.

"Funnily enough, there is no special name that I know of in the UK, though analysts do the calculation and examine the difference. They also calculate the relationship the other way round and call it percentage asset backing – perhaps this reflects the rather pessimistic view of analysts and bankers in the UK. They tend to distrust companies where the majority of the assets are intangible."

"How is this asset backing percentage calculated?" I reply. "I'm not sure what you mean."

She walks to the flipchart again.

"What were your asset figures – $180m?" I nod in

agreement. "Let's compare it with the bid price as I did yesterday."

	Per Share $	Total $m
Balance Sheet Book Value	18.36	180.000
Price	51	500.004
% Asset Backing	36%	36%

I look at this and it reminds me yet again how difficult it is for non-accountants like me when there are so many different ways of expressing the same figures. Yesterday it was 2.78 price to book, now it's 36% asset backing, both from the same two numbers. But, interestingly, the two ways of expressing it have helped me to appreciate the different ways it can be interpreted, depending on the perspective of the analyst.

"Chris," I say, "could we go back to the market price before the bid and see what it was then?"

"Sure," she says, "you calculate it for me." I hesitate but then remember that success in learning about finance is all about trying things and building confidence.

I take the figure of $18.36 assets per share and divide it into the pre-bid market price of $40 to get 45.9% or a price to book ratio of 2.18.

"Now Chris," I say, "can you tell me how the analysts would interpret these calculations?"

"Well they can only look at them in the context of a particular industrial sector. Obviously something like an advertising agency would have a high multiple and very little asset backing."

"Yes," I reply, "I can see that. So what are the implications of the way they are rated?"

"Well. The higher the price to book multiple, the higher the added value they've created so a high multiple is, in many ways, a compliment to the management and their perception by the outside world. It also means they're much less likely to be taken over because, as you'll see later, the goodwill has to be accounted for. But a high multiple also leaves them very vulnerable. Can you see why?"

I think back to the problems of large advertising agencies in recent times. How the image of the Saatchis suddenly changed almost overnight and how some agencies were hit by mass defections of their key staff. The share prices fell sharply because there were few assets to fall back on. I repeat this reasoning to Chris.

"Right," she confirms, showing pleasure at the way I seem to be grasping the issues, "the asset backing of a company should, in most cases, provide a minimum figure below which the share price should not fall, as long as the assets are reasonably capable of being realised if the business were to collapse. It's often more a psychological re-assurance than anything else – the analysts, particularly those from banks and credit agencies, like to see tangible asset values behind the share price."

"So Chapmans' – what was it – $18 per share asset value should be a level below which the share price could not fall, however badly it may be run."

"Should be, but you can never be sure," replies Chris, "a lot depends on the real, rather than book, values of assets and how feasible it would be for them to be sold if things went wrong. Indeed the minimum might be higher than $18 if there were valuable assets which would fetch more than their book value. Do you own this place for instance?"

She waves her hand towards the office and factory buildings outside the window behind my desk. I nod in confirmation.

"And when were they bought Phil?"

"I'm not sure – early 1960s I think. The book value is only a few hundred thousand dollars but we insure it for over $10 million."

"But what is the market value?"

"That I don't know. Depends on who bought it and for what purpose. It would be worth a fortune if permission were given for residential development."

"You see the problems of asset valuation Phil. In the UK, some firms revalue to market value but it's always a dodgy exercise. There was once a move to introduce replacement cost as a valuation method – which is almost certainly the basis of the 10 million dollars you quoted – but it was so difficult to implement consistently that they gave up. Historic cost is still the valuation method used most commonly. Despite all its imperfections, at least you can't argue with it."

Again I find myself becoming quite interested in the whole basis of accounting theory. Since I've had more direct involvement in the finance function these last four years, I've wanted to debate these issues with somebody but no-one's been around. I mention this to Chris.

"It's a big subject Phil, and I'd love to discuss it with you some time. But we have to think of priorities now and I'm not sure you can afford McKenzies' fees for a philosophical discussion about accounting – let's just try and focus on the things you need to know now."

"OK Chris. That's fine but maybe one of these days."

I think to myself that what I really want is her working for me again, as she did at Lawrensons, so I can then make any demands I want on her working time. But I guess that's a fantasy now, particularly as, one way or the other, Chapmans are likely to be taken over.

"Right Phil," she says in her usual businesslike way. "Now how much time have you got today? Can you carry on till lunchtime?"

"Unless I'm interrupted by Miles, yes," I reply, "but I need to be seen around the place this afternoon and it would be nice to see Karen and Tracy again before lunch. So let's finish around midday."

"Are you OK on the price to book ratio now?" she asks.

"Yes. But before we move on, tell me how Chapmans compares with other food companies. How did our multiple rate before the bid – 2.18 wasn't it?"

"That was about average but you should have been higher with your strong brands and Richard's good reputation in the business. Again it was your poor investor relations which dragged it down."

"But now, of course, we're over 3 at the latest price of $56."

"Because you're in play. People know you're going to

be sold for at least that price. If Richard had resigned before the Universal bid, the price could well have gone down."

"OK. Now while we're on the subject, let me get some of this jargon right. 'In play' means that people know you're a bid target and you're almost certain to go to one bidder or another. Right?"

"Yes Phil. There's a sort of inevitability about it once there's been a bid, unless there is some fundamental reason why a bid won't take place."

"Like a Poison Pill for instance?"

"Oh. That's been mentioned too has it?"

"Yes. Benetto suggested it but old George Chapman was violently against it. Tell me more about poison pills Chris."

"Well they are things which companies do to make themselves more difficult to swallow and thus avoid being taken over."

"Like for instance?"

"Contracts for excessive payoffs for Directors fired after a takeover – that's one. Another classic is paying a large dividend with borrowed money, thus creating high gearing for the acquirer to swallow. You remember gearing?"

"Of course Chris, though I have to call it leverage over here. I still remember your analogy with personal life – the person with high gearing is the one with the large mortgage. Any more poison pills?"

"There are various complex shareholding structures which can be created and which need lots of legal work to sort out – that's a huge deterrent over here with the high cost of lawyers' fees. Owning an insurance company has also proved to be very effective in the US – did you read about BAT's legal problems when they took over Farmers Insurance?"

"Yes. But didn't that serve them as a poison pill when Goldsmith made his bid for BAT?"

"Yes Phil. Quite right. I keep forgetting how far you've come since the Lawrenson days. Any other jargon?"

"White Knight is just a second bidder coming to the rescue?"

"Yes. After a hostile bid, a White Knight is the friendly bidder, either brought in or accepted by the victim. That's what you'll be getting by Monday unless I'm very much mistaken."

"You and Benetto both seem convinced," I say, "but I'm not so sure. Taking on Universal is not something which anyone with any sense would do, particularly when they're so determined to win."

"But, with management and family shareholders on their side, a White Knight can hardly fail Phil, as long as their bid is fair."

"We'll see," I say. "I've got this awful feeling that Universal are going to get us. Prior is not a man to back down easily."

Paul Prior was my boss during my latter period at Lawrensons and is now Universal's Director of US Operations. I've seen him twice since I came over to the States, in social situations, but never dreamt that he might ever be bidding for Chapmans. How naive and unprepared we were!

My brain is beginning to hurt but Chris is determined that I'm going to understand the importance of goodwill and its accounting treatment before the morning is out. I order another cup of coffee for us and she starts to explain, standing beside the flipchart as usual, looking totally enchanting. I know I'm falling for her all over again and I know I shouldn't but there's not a thing I can do about it.

"OK Phil," she says, oblivious to the emotions I'm feeling and looking as though accounting for goodwill is the only really important thing between us at this time. "The first thing to stress is that, when Universal acquire a company, that company's Balance Sheet becomes absorbed into the consolidated Universal Group Balance Sheet. OK?"

I nod in agreement because I know that already – I remember that Lawrensons effectively ceased to exist as a separate legal entity when they were acquired by Universal. It was the internal management accounts which were really important and any statutory figures were purely to comply with the minimum legal requirements.

"Now Phil, let's suppose that Universal buy Chapmans for their $500m bid and that your asset values stay at $180m. In practice Universal would probably agree higher asset values with their Auditors – they're allowed to negotiate a 'fair value' – whatever that means – because, as you'll see, this reduces the goodwill problem."

She writes up on the flipchart.

	Impact on Universal Balance Sheet
Universal pays to Chapman Shareholders	500m (Cash out)
And brings into the Consolidated Universal Balance Sheet assets of	180m (Assets in)
The balance must, initially, appear in the Balance Sheet as an asset	
i.e. GOODWILL of	320m

"You see Phil, if the Balance Sheet is to continue to balance, that $320m has to appear. But it is, in many ways, logical for it to appear because the company has purchased it from Chapman shareholders and it needs to be accounted for."

"But I'm still not happy about the label Chris – why is it called goodwill?"

"That's just a name Phil. I prefer to think of it as 'premium on acquisition'. The important thing is the impact on the Balance Sheet and the Earnings Per Share."

"But I'm still struggling with the concept Chris. What does it really represent?"

"Simply all the reasons why Universal are willing to pay $320m more than asset values to get hold of Chapmans. It will vary with each acquisition – it may be management expertise, market share, brands, opportunities to sell off separate businesses at a profit, potential cost savings and other synergy from combining with existing operations. We couldn't know Universal's justification for paying 500m unless we saw their plans for Chapmans and their internal calculations. But you can bet your life they've worked it through on a DCF basis and also calculated the impact on their EPS."

"I'd like to go through that with you sometime Chris, not necessarily Universal's but generally how a company would calculate the impact of an acquisition on its EPS."

"Maybe we'll do it on Monday for your White Knight," says Chris, smiling in anticipation at the thought, "but in the meantime there's this $320m in the Universal Balance Sheet, so what are they going to do with it?"

I decide I'll give her a surprise and I say in my best American accent, "I guess they'll amortise it."

She turns away in mock disgust. "I don't know why I'm bothering to explain all this when you seem to know it already. You're right – that's the American method. It's written off over a maximum of 40 years. They often use the phrase amortisation but you could just as well call it depreciation. So effectively it's accounted for in the same way as a tangible fixed asset."

"But what's the problem Chris? Why is there such controversy?"

"Because the British and most other European countries don't do it that way, as you'll see later. And just think about the impact on Earnings per Share as you charge $320m through your Profit and Loss Account as a write-off. Even over 40 years that's quite a hit."

"But I can't quite see the logic of writing it off at all Chris. Won't it be there for ever?"

"It depends. Would the Chapman brands survive long term within Universal? The management won't stay for ever and the benefit of the synergies will eventually be exhausted. Ultimately the new Chapmans within Universal would begin to renew and create its own goodwill. On balance I believe it should be written off but a number of US Chief Financial Officers share your view and would very much like to avoid the impact of amortisation on their EPS."

"Is that what the UK companies do? You said there was a significant difference."

"Not quite. They avoid the impact on EPS because the whole $320 million is written off in one year, against previous years' retained profits."

"You mean it's treated as a loss?"

"Effectively yes. There's a special entry reducing goodwill on the assets side and reducing retained profits (or reserves, remember, is the other term) on the other."

"That seems to fly in the face of reality Chris but I guess the UK Financial Directors don't mind."

"The UK accounting bodies claim that it follows the accounting convention of prudence," replies Chris, "but I tend to agree with you. It's pretending that something which has been bought for $320m doesn't exist and it allows the management to avoid accounting for it after that first year. But, surprisingly, the UK Financial Directors don't like their convention either – because it screws up their gearing. Now there's a good test for you – can you think why?"

I think back to when Chris first explained the gearing ratio to me. She said it was also called the debt/equity ratio and I've since discovered that the Americans also call it the leverage ratio. It is borrowing as a percentage of shareholders equity. Presumably borrowing could go up after an acquisition but not necessarily. Of course! The write-off of goodwill to reserves will reduce shareholders equity – the total of share capital plus reserves. I proudly relate this to Chris and she nods proudly too. We both feel very pleased with ourselves and with some justification. The financially illiterate Sales and Marketing Director of Lawrensons is now a Company President with reasonable financial competence. Even if he is only one small step ahead of events each time!

There's still one small gap in my knowledge. I look at my watch and see that we have 20 minutes or so to fill it.

"Now tell me about brands Chris – it was mentioned that some UK companies were showing brands in their Balance Sheet."

"Yes, that's right Phil. And it relates closely to what I've been saying. Because the whole goodwill situation has been chaotic with companies on both sides of the Atlantic saying that the other had an unfair advantage. The US complained about EPS and therefore share price, the UK about gearing. Some UK companies quoted on the US Stock Exchange produce two Annual Reports, one with each of the two different accounting treatments. Then Grand Metropolitan, a UK based company acquiring widely in the US, hit on a compromise which, they thought, achieved the best of both worlds. They found a consultancy who had developed a method for valuing brands based on a complex formula, involving market share, advertising spend, product life cycle etc. After an acquisition, they valued the acquired brands according to this formula and thus classified part of the goodwill as brands."

"And did they depreciate, sorry amortise, them?"

"Not immediately. They agreed with their Auditors to review the brand values each year and only write them down if events proved them to be worth less."

"That's interesting Chris," I reply. "It seems that the Auditors have a crucial role, far more than I appreciated before. So what's the state of play in the goodwill stakes now?"

"Chaotic. The UK accounting bodies are reconsidering their position, some companies are following Grand Met, others are going over to the US system but with lower write-off periods. It's a bit of a shambles."

"And Universal? What do they do?"

"They've so far followed the UK convention and have always written goodwill off to reserves. That's why their gearing has increased these last two years. It was over 100% last year. But it's possible they may change their accounting methods next year and go for the Grand Met or US method."

"So that's it on brands?" I ask hopefully but suspect that I could be disappointed. And I'm right.

Chris has a final postscript.

"There has been one more development about brands which you might as well know about," she continues.

"Some companies jumped on the bandwagon and used the same method to value, and bring into the Balance Sheet, brands which have not been acquired but have just been developed over the years. Which raises those same issues about the Balance Sheet's function all over again – whether it can and should ever be a valuation statement of all assets. And yes Phil, I promise I'll discuss that when we've more time, on an informal basis if necessary. Although I'm still a management accountant at heart, I find these financial accounting issues fascinating too and they really can have a big impact on management decisions."

I can't close the discussion until I've settled one nagging doubt in my mind.

"Chris," I say, "I'm sure there's a simple answer but how does the Balance Sheet still balance after a brand valuation like the one you've just described is brought into the Balance Sheet?"

"Phil," she says with a smile which again reminds me how hopelessly infatuated I am with her, "you're a true accountant at heart. It's like a property revaluation – a special revaluation reserve is created so it's the reverse of a goodwill write-off. It boosts shareholders equity and helps gearing. That's why some companies like to do it. And they also hope that publishing their brand values will boost their share price though I'm not sure the analysts are always impressed by it. They see it as creative accounting and I think they're right."

I'd like to discuss creative accounting further because I've often heard the term without really understanding it. But it's midday and our time is up. I sit back and look at her, hoping that my true feelings aren't showing too obviously. At some point I'm going to have to say how I feel but not today.

Suddenly the door bursts open and Miles comes in. He smiles at Chris and says, "Hi, you must be Christine, good to meet you, I'm Miles Chapman."

Without waiting for Chris to reply, he turns to me and says, "Phil, I've just had a call from my broker. Chapmans have hit 60 on rumours of a bid from Royston. He reckons there's been an inspired leak from somewhere – I can't understand why Benetto hasn't told us. Could you get him on the phone?"

As he says this the phone rings. It's Tracy. "Paul Benetto's on the line for you Phil," she says.

Chapter 9

It's Sunday afternoon and it's a beautiful day, very warm for the middle of May. I'm sitting by the side of our swimming pool watching my children cavorting in and out of the water, accompanied apparently by half the children in the neighbourhood. I ought to be relaxing without a care in the world but I'm not. Try as I may, I just can't get the Universal takeover out of my mind though the several glasses of Californian Chablis which I've taken with my lunch are making it easier to do so.

I'm beginning to see how unpredictable these takeover battles can be. There was great excitement when the leak about Royston's bid came out and when the share price rose to $60. Paul Benetto warned us to be careful not to expect too much because his view was that Universal may have inspired the leak. Their motive could be to put Royston on the spot, create shareholder expectations and then be well placed for a second 'knock-out' bid on Monday.

If this was Universal's strategy, it seemed to be working because, just before Wall Street closed, Royston put out a statement saying they were not bidding for Chapmans and the price fell back to $57. We all went away for the weekend in a state of depression, convinced that Universal will bid on Monday at a level which shareholders will not be able to refuse, somewhere around the $60 mark.

Jean is lying back on the reclining chair next to me, a

glass of wine in her hand too. She looks relaxed though I know she's been badly hit by Richard and Barbara's breakup, spending most of yesterday trying to console her. Sorry though I am for Barbara, I must confess to being pleased that she refused our invitation to spend today with us.

I find it hard to understand why they cannot get together again. Richard has apparently been offered the chance to set up a new operation for a Canadian investment company entering the UK and it sounds like just the opportunity he needs. After her first impulsive reaction to him leaving Chapmans, Barbara now wants him back but isn't prepared to uproot the family by moving back to the UK. And Richard seems to be saying – for once in my life I'm going to do what I want to do and to hell with everyone else. I tried to contact him yesterday without success; no-one seems to know where he is. I'm seriously concerned at his state of mind – it's amazing for me to feel this about a man who, only last weekend, I thought to be the epitome of stability and common sense.

I decide that the time is right for me to tell Jean about Chris's new role at Chapmans. There'll never be a better opportunity.

"Darling," I say, "there's something I've been meaning to tell you but it's been so hectic this week."

"Hmm," she says, and I look across to see that her eyes are closing as she lies back in the sun. But I persevere.

"You remember Christine Goodhart who was at Lawrensons?"

"Hmm," she replies, but suddenly sits up, wide awake, looking towards me. No chance of slipping this one through quietly I think.

"Of course I remember her Phil," she replies. "Why? Have you met up with her again?"

The words seem harmless enough but already I sense from her voice that she's concerned.

"Yes," I reply, trying my best to sound casual, "she's working for McKenzies, the management consultants. In fact she's helping us with the takeover."

Jean sits up even further and leans towards me.

"Really?" she says with a tone which seems to contain a combination of sarcasm and resignation, "and who brought her in then? You I suppose."

"Yes I did love but it's strictly business, honestly. We're both clear about that. And, now I'm President, I really have to have someone to advise me on financial issues and she really is superb at that. You don't mind do you?"

I already know the answer from the tone of her voice and the look on her face. But it wouldn't be like Jean to come out with it openly.

"I suppose not," she says, getting up to walk away. "You must do what you think best. But you be careful Philip Moorley, you be careful."

Her voice falters as she says this and I can sense the emotion she's feeling. She always did know my motives and my weaknesses better than I did and maybe she's sharing some of this feeling of inevitability that's been with me ever since I saw Chris again. I think I see tears in Jean's eyes as she gets up and walks away to sit by the poolside close to the children. I know from past experience that it's not worth discussing the matter further until she's calmed down.

I'm just pouring myself another glass of Chablis when Mark, my son, shouts from the house: "Dad, telephone for you."

"Who is it?"

"Mr Chapman."

I get up, thinking how unusual it is for Miles to be working over the weekend and how important it must be for him to ring me on a Sunday. I decide not to use the portable phone but go inside to my study.

"Hi Miles," I say.

"Hi Phil. Sorry to disturb you on a Sunday but things are happening. I've been contacted by Arnold Kaufman, Chairman of ABT and he wants to discuss their position today. And we both want you to be involved. Can you come over to my place?"

"Sure Miles, give me an hour. Do you think we should contact Paul Benetto?"

"Well ABT want it to be informal at this stage so I

wouldn't want him to attend this meeting. But maybe we should tell him and ask his advice."

"I think we should Miles. We really have to be very careful. We're both novices at this game and ABT are very experienced operators."

An hour later I'm entering the sweeping drive of Miles's 'place' – a mansion which makes my dream house seem very small beer indeed. He's always complaining about the cost of running it and paying off the bank loan, but I guess that will no longer be a problem once he's sold out his shareholding in Chapmans.

Benetto was pleased that ABT had approached us but a little concerned at our meeting Kaufman alone. He stressed the need to hold back from making any firm commitment until he's had time to advise us and all the options are on the table. I promised him that I would do everything I could to leave all options open.

As I get out of my car, Miles is already outside the house and greets me warmly. Again I feel good about the way we're working together and generally getting on. Before we go in I repeat what Benetto has advised and Miles replies, "I know Phil. I realise that and Kaufman appreciates it too. This is off the record and we have all the options open tomorrow. But there is one thing you ought to know before we go in."

"What's that Miles?"

"That Kaufman has met Richard this morning. Somehow he tracked him down and tried to persuade him to change his mind about leaving. I'd already told Kaufman that I'd rather have you now anyway but Richard's reputation in the industry is very high."

"And what did Richard say?"

"Apparently he was most unhelpful and said he was through working for big US corporations. Something about going to start a business in the UK. From what Kaufman said, he seems to be in a poor state."

He then adds, as we walk through the house, "So a lot hangs on you giving the right impression here Phil. ABT want to buy Chapmans as an ongoing business which is what most of the family shareholders want too."

My mind's in a whirl as I walk into Miles's living room and see Arnold Kaufman standing there. I know exactly what is at stake – my career, the jobs of many people at Chapmans, the future of the business as a separate entity. Benetto has already told me how ABT, unlike Universal, claim to allow a high degree of autonomy to their operating company managers. As a policy, they never consider hostile takeovers as they seek continuity and management stability after their acquisitions.

Kaufman greets me with a friendly smile. He's a bit like a caricature of the elderly, American businessman – white-haired, distinguished and avuncular. I think to myself that he's been through this routine many times before and, if he's Chairman of ABT, he's not going to be fooled by bullshit. I decide I'll play it straight down the middle.

Miles asks Kaufman to start the meeting and state his position to both of us. I wonder to myself what the two of them have discussed before I arrived. Who is working with whom?

"Now Phil, I hope you don't mind me being informal, please call me Arnold. I'll come straight to the point – I'm not one to beat about the bush. We want to come to an arrangement with the Chapman shareholders about bringing your company into the ABT Group. But we won't do so unless we're sure that you and your management team are behind us. Do you understand me?"

"Yes sir," I reply, regretting the fact that my conservative English upbringing still makes me unable to call him Arnold this quickly, "I know that this is your policy and I understand it fully. But I'm surprised you weren't put off by Richard's departure."

"I was put off, I will admit that. But Miles here persuaded me that you have many of the same qualities and a few that Richard hasn't got too. In particular he tells me that, for a sales and marketing man, you have an astute financial brain. That's pretty important to ABT."

As he says this I realise yet again how much my career has benefited from the time at Lawrensons when Chris helped me free my mental block about financial understanding. It seems that, in many companies, in many countries, a manager with good financial awareness is likely to be well placed when opportunities arise. And however insecure I may still be about my knowledge, it's better than most and it's increasing all the time.

Meanwhile Kaufman is going on at length about his company's values and philosophies. Like most people at that level, he loves the chance to talk about his company but I feel that there's a lot of sincerity too. He does seem to care about his people and about society, the latter perhaps an attempt to redress the balance for the fact that his company was built on the back of vast amounts of money made from the tobacco industry. In response to my question about this, he admits that nearly 50% of profits still come from these activities.

He tells me how Chapmans would operate within the ABT group. He claims that it would carry on much as at present. ABT like to operate as a shareholder, letting the management get on with running the business, being judged on financial results.

"Would you put any of your management into the Company?" I ask, knowing that Universal always did just that, very soon after acquisition.

"You will have a new Chairman, Phil and that will be one of our Main Board. Miles here has made it quite clear that he doesn't want to be directly involved with Chapmans but will join the ABT Board in a non-executive capacity. We would like to put in a Chief Financial Officer because we have our own accounting control systems which are very important. They are the basis on which our companies are allowed autonomy – complete freedom as long as you deliver the agreed financial results and that needs good accounting reports each month using methods which are unique to ABT."

"So I could keep the management team apart from the new CFO?"

"Yes."

"And could I appoint two new VPs, one for sales and one for marketing to replace the job I used to do?"

"If that's what you want Phil yes."

"And what about the Controller I have now? Would he

be able to stay?"

"That's up to you Phil. You'll need to discuss it with your new CFO but I'm sure a role could be found for him. Then you'll have to decide if you can afford him and still deliver the required results which you'll agree with your new Chairman."

I like the sound of this and tell him so. I hope that I'm in a strong enough position to push for one more concession, one that has suddenly occurred to me and which makes the prospect of a future within ABT even more rosy.

"Arnold," I say, at last finding the confidence to use his first name, "I know that I need a new CFO, particularly if we are to become part of the ABT Group. But would you consider someone from outside? Someone who, I can promise you, would be an asset to ABT? She's worked with me before and she now works with McKenzies. I can assure you she's the best. A qualified accountant in the UK and a Harvard MBA."

"I can't promise but I should think the chances are high if she's that good. Our Group CFO is always complaining about the poor supply of good financial people and if she's that good and she'll leave McKenzies for our compensation package, I think it should be OK. Do you think she'll join us?"

"I believe so," I say as convincingly as I can, despite having absolutely no logical reason to think that. But something inside tells me that she will.

"Could you please tell me more about your proposed bid for Chapmans Arnold?" I say. "We're talking as if it's already happened but surely there's a long way to go yet."

I sit back waiting for him to tell me about their offer, confident that my recent sessions with Chris will help me to understand and analyse the financial implications.

"OK Phil," he says, "let me tell you what we have in mind. First thing to say is that a cash bid is out of the question for ABT. Our cash resources are already committed to investing in our existing businesses and we have a policy of keeping below a leverage of 50% debt to equity, which we're slightly over at present. So this arrangement has to be by the issue of new shares which will also offer tax advantages for some of the Chapmans shareholders. Thus it's even more important for Chapmans to run effectively within ABT because Chapmans shareholders are taking ABT shares as the consideration for the deal. You get me?"

"Sure," I say confidently, but inside feeling slightly panicky, knowing that I am running into new uncharted territory.

"We're offering two ABT shares for every three Chapmans," continues Kaufman. "Now ABT were quoted on Friday at $93 so that values Chapmans at $62. But all depends on how the bid is received by the Market – hence I need you guys to be totally supportive. One problem is that our P/E is down to about 9 while this bid gives Chapmans an exit P/E of 19 historic and 17 prospective. Now I'm confident that the potential of Chapmans and the strong brands you've built up will eventually justify that rating. But I'm very worried about the impact on our share price once the announcement is made."

Every time I think I've got a financial topic cracked, something else comes along to remind me how much I still have to learn. Share for share deals are obviously a whole new ball game.

Miles comes in with a question which tells me that even he understood Kaufman's comments better than I did.

"But surely Arnold," he says, "Chapmans aren't that big within ABT to have a major impact on EPS are they?"

"Well historic earnings are about $32 million and you've now announced a forecast of $35 million for this year. Our profits this year are just over $200 million so you're by no means insignificant. And the analysts regard our move into foods as crucial to the quality of our future earnings so they'll be doing their own calculations. I've got our financial boys working on our EPS model today and they'll have all the data for the analysts once we announce the bid. What we want to avoid is our price dropping on the announcement."

I change the subject to safer ground, resolving that I must get Chris to explain all this to me at our meeting tomorrow.

"But aren't Universal going to come in with a higher bid tomorrow?" I ask, looking at both Miles and Arnold.

"That's likely," says Miles, "but, if we announce this proposal with full support of the family, the other major shareholders and the management by lunchtime tomorrow, we think Universal will bow out."

"I think we ought to talk to Paul Benetto about that," I say, "he's not so sure that Universal will wait till lunchtime or will back out that easily.   Remember the UK is five hours ahead of us. What if Universal come in with a bid at $65 or so?"

"At $65 we have no chance Philip," says Arnold with a resigned smile.   "I'm afraid that if they're prepared to go that far you'll end up working for Universal."

Chapter 10

"Phil, you mustn't panic about these things," says Chris the next morning as I'm telling her about the ABT deal. "The detail is complicated but the principle is not. If ABT are paying a high price for Chapmans and they're issuing shares as a consideration, a lot of ABT shares are going to have to be issued. So it's hardly surprising that they're worried about the impact on their EPS is it?"

As usual, when Chris explains things, they don't seem quite so complex any more. I now recall reading in the UK about companies like Saatchi and Gateway Supermarkets who had severe problems because they paid high prices for acquisitions and issued too many shares to pay for them. Diluting their EPS, as Benetto called it earlier this morning and, in the process, driving down the share price.

"Shall we have a look at the sort of calculation which ABT and the Wall Street analysts will be making Phil?" asks Chris.

I look at my watch and see that it's nearly midday – I've managed to snatch this session with Chris after a long morning meeting with Miles and Paul Benetto. They've now gone their separate ways to consult family, Board and other shareholders while I brief the other executive VPs. So far there is no news from Universal and we hope to announce the ABT proposal soon after lunch. Benetto's view is that, as long as the ABT share price holds, it should be a winning bid unless Universal come in with significantly more and still retain the offer of a cash alternative.

It will, he said this morning, be very hard to persuade shareholders to accept the uncertainty of a share for share deal if Universal are offering a higher price and the certainty of cash too. Recent experience of share for share offers on Wall Street has apparently been bad – share prices have fallen even further than initial estimates because large numbers of new shareholders sell after the deal goes through to realise cash. Benetto mentioned this as yet another reason why the ABT bid has to be sold to all shareholders – hence the need for him and Miles to do some effective lobbying this morning.

"Shall we carry on Phil?" says Chris, seeing my uncertainty.

"Yes," I reply, "at least for the time being, until we're interrupted by Miles or Paul. There may be meetings with ABT later on today and I'd like to understand this fully before then – particularly as their Chairman seems to think I have an astute financial brain!"

I relayed most of the detail of the previous day's meeting to Chris earlier on and, though we laughed about Kaufman's praise of my financial acumen, deep down we were both pretty pleased with ourselves. It was good to share with her the pride in my increased knowledge and to see how important it really can be. The one thing I haven't mentioned to Chris is the rather reckless request I made to Kaufman about her joining Chapmans as CFO. I will have to leave that until later.

I've also not told Chris about Jean's reaction to the news of her working with me again – I'm sure she'd be concerned if she knew. Jean was very cold and distant when I returned late from Miles' place and, unusually for us, we went to sleep without talking things through. I am now deeply involved with Chris and know that I'm jeopardising my marriage by having her around but, when I'm here with her like this, there seems to be no alternative.

Chris walks over to her briefcase and picks out two copies of the ABT Annual Report.

"OK Phil," she says, "let's write up the current ABT

market capitalisation. I've checked that they've not issued further shares since last year's accounts. There's 21 million shares in issue."

She writes up:

Shares Issued	Share Price today	Market Cap.
21m	$93	$1953m

and then adds:

EARNINGS	$9.76 (per share) $205m (total)

"Just a minute Chris," I say. "Where have the earnings figures come from?"

"In the Profit and Loss Account – sorry Income Statement as they call it over here. Page 32, two lines from the bottom – net earnings of $205m. The EPS figure is shown on the last line but you can also get $9.76 by dividing $205m by 21m shares – OK?"

I understand this and in a much more confident and lasting way than last week. As I found at Lawrensons when looking at management accounting – the more you work on these things the easier they become. Once you break the mental block, the learning curve is very steep.

"So can you see the P/E Phil?" asks Chris.

"Of course," I say, "it's between 9 and 10 – about 9.5 I think. Nine was the figure which Kaufman quoted to me yesterday. But why is it so low Chris?"

"It's a lot to do with the sector they're in Phil. Although they've diversified, they're still regarded as a tobacco company and I think it's still about half their profits. And there are poor growth prospects in tobacco and a very uncertain future what with all the health problems and, in ABT's case, some legal claims in prospect. So they're not going to be rated highly. The one thing that prevents the price going even lower is their high dividend payout and I think they might say something about dividend when they announce the bid."

"Sorry Chris. Could you explain that. We didn't cover dividends last week if you remember."

"Right. Well, ABT have tried over the years to compensate their shareholders for lack of share price growth with a relatively high dividend and they could afford to do this because of the positive cash flow from their tobacco operations. But now they have little cash left for new acquisitions. They only cover the dividend 1.7 times which is lower than average. Remember that low cover means high payout. A dividend cover under 2 is regarded as quite low. Let me write this up."

She writes under the earnings figure:

	Per Share	Total
EARNINGS	$9.76	$205m
DIVIDEND	$5.76	$121m
DIVIDEND COVER	1.7	

"You see Phil, 9.76 divided by 5.76 gives you the cover – or you can also get it by dividing the totals – 205m by 121m. The totals are usually more easily available in the accounts. Dividend cover is used in the UK Stock Exchange but, over here, they often reverse the calculation and talk about dividend payout ratio – that would be 5.76 as a percentage of 9.76 ...59%. It's just another way of expressing the same concept."

"Right, but what do they mean when they talk about dividend yield?"

"The yield is the percentage cash return shareholders are getting at today's market price. So if the price is $93 and the cash return is 5.76, this will be a return of just over 6%," she checks her calculator, "6.19% to be precise."

"Which is high?"

"Sure. Because it has both the features which create a high yield. A low price and therefore low P/E but a high cash payout. It's an ideal stock for an investor who wants a good cash return but is prepared to accept limited prospects for growth."

"And buying Chapmans will help them to achieve better prospects of growth?"

"Yes. That's what their whole diversification policy is about. Food manufacture is believed to have that nice combination of growing markets, relative stability and the prospect of improved margins. That's why the average P/E is higher than the tobacco sector."

"But why do you say that ABT may say something about dividend when they announce their bid?"

"Because, with all the new shares they're going to issue, there may be some concerns among existing shareholders about whether dividend per share can be held. Let's have a look at the new shares which will have to be issued according to the figures Kaufman gave you. I'm not yet sure how significant the dilution of dividend and earnings per share is likely to be."

She then writes up:

ABT Shares now issued	21.0m
Chapman shares now issued 9.804	
ABT new shares – 2 for every 3 Chapmans	6.54m
Total ABT shares after acquisition	27.54m

"Is that OK Phil?" asks Chris, stepping back from the flipchart and leaning on the edge of my desk.

I nod in agreement – this part at least seems straightforward. Chapman share certificates will be cancelled and every shareholder will get two ABT shares for every three Chapmans, hence the bid valuation which Kaufman quoted of $62 – two thirds of the present price of $93.

"Now," continues Chris, "let's have a look at the combined earnings and the new EPS."

She then writes up:

ABT Earnings	205m
Chapman Earnings	32m
Combined Earnings	237m
Combined Shares	27.54m
EPS after acquisition	$8.61

"So you see Phil," says Chris, looking again at the ABT Annual Report, "this compares with the current EPS of $9.76 so it's a significant dilution. Let's have a look at the dividend position. If they hold their dividend per share on the new holding they'll pay $5.76 on 27.54m shares – that's – where's my calculator – 158.6m dividend out of 237m earnings – the cover's reduced to 1.49 – that's quite significant too."

"Now slow down Chris, slow down please," I plead. "I can see how you calculated the $8.61 – 237 divided by 27.54 – but I can't see why it's down so much and what that means. Please could you go over that again for me."

"Sorry Phil. I get carried away with these calculations because I always find the numbers in share for share acquisitions so fascinating. I did a lot of this work during my time in Wall Street. The reason the EPS is so much down is because of the high valuation of Chapmans – the $62 price and the exit P/E of – what is it? – $62 divided by EPS of $3.28 – nearly 19."

I'm at least comfortable with those figures because I've now worked out the Chapmans P/E ratio as just about every price between 40 and 65 but I still have problems relating the exit P/E to the impact on ABT's earnings per share. I mention this point to Chris.

"But can't you see Phil, the exit P/E determines the number of shares to be issued and the extent of dilution. If the bid had been valued at, say, $46 that would have been only one ABT share for two Chapmans and there would have been far less shares around to dilute the earnings per share."

Again it all clicks into place for me and I feel that I'm really getting there at last. But I'm still not absolutely certain about the impact on share price.

"So are you saying that the ABT price will fall now or later?"

"Well that's the unknown element Phil. One thing's for sure – if it's likely to fall later, it will fall now because the analysts will be doing the calculations we've just done as soon as the bid is announced. The key question is – can the market be convinced that the combined Chapmans/ABT operation deserves a higher P/E than ABT had before because that's what it needs to hold the share price at its pre-bid level. That's where ABT's reputation and investor relations are put to the test. That's why it's so important to announce a bid that has full management support and a logical strategy behind it. Otherwise the P/E will not improve and the price will fall. I would imagine that they'll announce prospective earnings in both cases."

"Slow down again Chris please, one thing at a time. Show me what you mean about the P/E on a flipchart please."

She writes up:

	$
Combined Earnings per Share after Acquisition	8.61
Price now	93
P/E needed to maintain present share price	10.8
Price if present P/E of 9.5 is not improved	82

Looking at these figures, I'm surprised how significant the impact of the Chapmans acquisition on ABT is likely to be. And the reason is the high price paid for Chapmans and the high exit P/E, particularly in relation to ABT's low rating. Thus the P/E has to be 'talked up' as Benetto said over the phone this morning though I wasn't quite sure what he meant at the time. I'm not quite certain about the 82 figure and ask Chris to go through that again.

"Well the P/E of ABT now is 9.5 – the present price of 93 divided by the present EPS of 9.76. If the market is not convinced that ABT will generate better EPS growth with Chapmans than it is now doing without them, the P/E will not rise. And the price will fall to $82, 8.61 multiplied by the existing P/E of 9.5."

"And is that likely?"

"I would hope not because, if it does, the bid is probably scuppered. Chapmans shareholders will relate their two for three offer to the new price so it would only be worth what – about $54 or $55 – which is below their present market price."

"So the price of ABT's shares now becomes the key variable. I now see why the Guinness share price was so important in the Distillers bid and why their takeover team were so keen to support it. Presumably these share support operations happen where the price begins to fall and they try to prevent it by getting people to buy the shares?"

"Right Phil. That's it absolutely. But I hope it won't be necessary here. Announcing prospective earnings, making favourable noises about ABT's results this year and perhaps hinting about synergies with their existing food operations will all help. And, as I mentioned, confirming continuation of the dividend per share will also help because that high yield – what was it? 6.2% – is bound to be attractive to shareholders who are keen to have cash income rather than long-term capital gain."

"Yes," I reply, "tell me more about the dividend because I didn't totally follow the point you made earlier."

"Have we got time Phil?" she says, looking tiredly at her watch. "Don't you want to check the position with Miles or Paul? And I'm hungry."

I see that it's gone 12.30pm. I've been so involved that I've hardly noticed the time or my own need for food.

"Sorry Chris," I say feeling guilty, "I'll get some sandwiches sent in and don't worry about Miles and Paul.

They'll interrupt me if anything new has broken. But I would imagine they'll be tied up over lunch and report back afterwards."

She sits back in the chair across the other side of my desk, by the side of the flipchart. She stifles a yawn.

"Sorry Phil," she says, "I'm finding this quite exhausting and I had a rather hectic weekend. I remember from Lawrensons how tiring these kind of sessions were for both of us."

I want to ask her precisely what her hectic weekend consisted of, who she was with and what she was doing. But I don't for two reasons. For one thing I want to cover all the financial factors surrounding the bid while there's time and secondly I know I'll sound like a jealous lover. Because that's precisely how I feel! Her stunning looks combined with her outstanding knowledge and confidence for one so young, completely bowl me over. I try to remember what her age is – must be close to thirty now – still just about young enough to be my daughter. Is it all a middle-aged fantasy? But then I think of that day at Heathrow Airport when she first went to the States. "I thought you were fantastic from the first time I saw you," she told me and I've treasured the memory of those words ever since. It's the thought of them that seems to be driving me away from my family and everything I've valued so much during the last four years that Jean and I have been together again.

"OK," she says, "let's have a quick look at the dividend position before the food comes in."

	Per Share	Total
Present ABT Earnings	$9.76	$205m
Present ABT Dividend	$5.76	$121m
Dividend Cover	1.7	1.7
Combined Historic Earnings after Chapmans acquisition	$8.61	$237m

"Now those shareholders seeking income will be hoping for a continuation of a dividend per share of at least 5.76, even after the EPS dilution. If the cover of 1.7 stayed the same, the payout would only be $8.61 divided by 1.7 – which is – just over $5. So to pay out $5.76 the cover will need to reduce to about 1.5 or whatever 8.61 divided by 5.76 gives you."

"Will that matter?"

"Probably not though it is a high payout for a US company and it could cause questions to be asked about whether enough funds are being ploughed back for the future. But again ABT will probably quote prospective earnings and imply that, by the next payout, EPS will have increased enough to pay at least the same dividend, maybe even more, and still retain the cover."

I'm beginning to feel exhausted too – I know from past experience how easy it is to reach saturation point and that's usually a good time to stop. I ask one further question – her view of the likely impact of the bid announcement on the shares of both Chapmans and ABT.

"I can't be sure Phil," she says patiently. "If I could predict prices that well, I wouldn't need to work for McKenzies. I'd be living in luxury in the Caribbean somewhere. But Chapmans will almost certainly go to around $62 because, however ABT's case is received, the price will be underpinned by the prospect of a second Universal bid, at least for the time being. But ABT – I just don't know. The analysts have a lot of respect for ABT's financial acumen and ABT's own financial people will be producing EPS projections – I'd be surprised if it falls much below its present price of $93; if it does we've got problems."

"We've got problems? Does 'we' include you?"

"Yes, I guess so. I feel very committed to Chapmans and to you Phil – I really hope the deal with ABT goes through. Though I still think you'd be OK with Universal anyway – they weren't that bad you know. You seemed to get on fine at Lawrensons. I know they're fairly controlling and they've become more so since they decided they needed this global approach to marketing but there are plenty worse. And I'd be very surprised if you were to lose your job at Chapmans. Universal are always looking for high calibre managers and that's what you are if only you had the confidence to recognise it."

I smile across my desk at her, remembering how she always had that wonderful knack of saying things that would be patronising from anyone else in a way which you can't help but accept. But the time is not right to raise the matter of the CFO job. No point in offering something that may never materialise. There would certainly be little chance of persuading Universal to take on Chris – their own financial person would be in Chapmans within days.

"Are share for share acquisitions always this complicated?" I ask, deciding that it's best to change the subject.

"Believe it or not Phil, this one is simple because it's totally share for share. Actually the cash bids or those funded by borrowing are often more difficult to predict because you have to make assumptions about the impact of interest costs on earnings. And those which involve a combination of cash and shares get even more complex. The worst of all is where there's some kind of convertible bonds – these are borrowings bearing interest initially but convertible into ordinary stock at some agreed future date. That's when the computer models are really important – they need to calculate EPS on various assumptions about conversion rates and times. They also calculate a fully diluted EPS – what it would be if all options to convert were taken up."

"In that case I'm grateful that ABT's gearing was too high for anything but a share for share bid. I couldn't really have taken any more this morning."

The phone rings and makes us both jump. I pick it up and Carl is on the line.

"Phil," he says, "there's another fax come in from Universal. Shall I bring it in?"

"You bet!" I say and feel my heart pound.

Two minutes later I'm reading a letter from Paul Prior, the man who used to terrify me when he was my boss at Universal. I scan over the preliminary words and my eyes focus on the really important part.

"Cash bid of $61.20, valuing Chapmans at $600million. A press release will be put out at 6.00 pm UK time."

I look at my watch and see that it's 1.05 pm, 5 minutes after the press release. I pick up the phone and ask Tracy to try and locate Miles and Paul.

"$61 Chris – it'll be touch and go but I think we're going to make it."

PART TWO

FIGHTING FOR SURVIVAL

Chapter 11

"Phil," says Matt Talbot, with a smile which has more than a trace of menace in it, "I'm afraid that this kind of result just isn't good enough in ABT. After these special adjustments for depreciation and interest costs, you don't even make a profit at all. You'd better start working with that new CFO of yours to improve things or I see nothing but trouble ahead."

Matt Talbot is ABT's 'Coordinator of Worldwide Food Operations', the new Chairman of Chapmans and my boss since we became part of ABT only six months ago. I still remember vividly the rejoicing that greeted the news that Universal had accepted defeat. They saw that there was no chance of forcing their bid through against the wishes of a united Chapman family shareholding, a number of major shareholders and a management team committed to ABT.

As I sit looking dismally at the special profitability report which ABT require us to prepare each month, I know that I, for one, am having a few doubts about that commitment and most of my team share them. Only Christine, now installed as my Chief Financial Officer – a source of continuous joy and surprise to me – seems to be enjoying life, maybe because she didn't know what Chapmans was like before the ABT acquisition.

The Chapman shareholders must be wondering if they made the right choice too. ABT's shares have fallen from $93 to only $80, largely on adverse publicity about even more litigation from relatives of those who've died through smoking. The shareholders must be wishing they'd taken the $61 cash alternative which Universal offered – only those who sold their ABT shares quickly (and contributed to the price fall) are laughing now.

Talbot gets up to go and tells me that he'll see me next week – all Arnold Kaufman's talk about leaving their companies alone to run their own operations seems very far away now. When I saw Kaufman at an ABT function last week he told me it was to do with financial results – get those right and you'll be left alone. I always thought Chapmans was pretty profitable but apparently not by ABT methods and standards.

I'm still having problems understanding these, in fact Christine has promised to go through them again with me when Talbot has gone. Her joining Chapmans has really been the one bright spot in my working life during these last six months. Her contributions to management meetings, her constant advice on the financial implications of decisions, her willingness to act as tutor and sounding board, have all helped me immensely. If our relationship could have stayed like that, maybe it would have been better but, quite recently, we have started an affair, something which I suspect is known by all those close to us at Chapmans. I'm also sure it's known by Jean too, though we've never discussed it openly. It's just that things aren't the same, in and out of bed, and she's already getting suspicious of my erratic hours. This last week it's been much easier because Jean's taken the children back to the UK for a visit to grandparents but I know there's no future in the present situation. I'm still very torn – the excitement of the conquest and our first sexual encounters was just wonderful and a great boost to my ego but now the secrecy and the uncertainty are taking the edge off it. And, despite my infatuation with Chris, I still don't feel sure I can make the break and destroy my marriage again.

As Chris walks into my office, happy and smiling, I wonder about her underlying feelings. I still find it hard to understand why someone so young and attractive should want to have an affair with me but she seems very relaxed, showing none of the sort of pressure which I am feeling. She's never talked about the future and never shown any sign that she wants more than we have now. The only sign of concern is that, ever since we started our affair, she's insisted on an agreement not to mention Jean or the children. I find this difficult but I guess it's best for both of us.

Our working relationship has not been affected at all and I hope this is a tribute to both of us and our commitment to getting things right at Chapmans. Her arrival has taken an enormous load off me and the appointment of Jane and Henry as VPs, has, so far, been very successful. The other two VPs, John Madden, Production and Al Morton, Personnel, have also been marvellous and I'm extremely lucky to have such an able management team. We have had some trouble with Carl who feels that his job as Controller has been devalued by Chris's appointment (which of course it has), but I have confidence that Chris will win him over.

The problem is that, however good I think the team is, ABT are not satisfied with the results according to their special methods of accounting, and this is why Chris is going to explain them to me today. She sits down by the side of me at the big oak table which I use for meetings – I've decided that looking across at people over a desk creates too much of a barrier. As I describe my meeting with Talbot, she nods from time to time but does not seem to share my anger and frustration.

"They have a point Phil and the methods they use aren't that unusual. They also have some logic and justification, even if they don't tie in with normal accounting principles."

"OK, but just explain to me what the main adjustments are and why the impact is so enormous. As far as I can see they convert a return on capital of over 20% to a loss."

She gets up from the table and walks towards the window. She sees someone in the car park outside and waves to them – I've been most impressed by the way she's become so popular very quickly. I guess that's not too surprising in view of her looks and personality – the sales team have been drooling over her since the moment she joined us. Yet I'm the one she's having the affair with, I think to myself in a rather smug and childish way. And there's no doubt it was what she wanted on that day, two months ago, when it all started, a month after she joined Chapmans. I may have suggested the drink together after we'd been working on a price revision all day but Chris suggested it should be at her apartment and, from that moment, there was no going back.

She turns round and faces me, looking undecided.

"I'm just wondering if we ought to go back to basic principles Phil. Your financial knowledge on the management accounting side is really good though I still have areas I would like to cover with you and which we'll need to apply if we're going to turn this business round. But, when we were together at Lawrensons, we never really covered financial accounting principles and conventions. And you really need this now because ABT's methods do bring out some fundamental issues about the whole purpose of accounting."

She walks towards the flipchart by the table and adds, "But we'll need a little while and may have to carry on another day. I've got a meeting at 4.00 pm. How are you fixed?"

I tell her that I've no more appointments today and she carries on.

"OK Phil, now let's go back a bit. At Lawrensons you discovered the Profit and Loss Account and Balance Sheet and what they told you about the business. Can you recall what we agreed as their basic purpose?"

"The Profit and Loss Account is to measure trading performance and to report to shareholders and others on how well the business is being run."

"Right. Because looking at cash generation is, in the short term and on its own, not necessarily a good measure of performance. You need to look at what is being sold and what is being spent to run the business in a particular period. The difference between the two is profit which provides a good indicator of management performance. Now tell me what is the Balance Sheet's purpose."

"It lists the assets which the business owns."

"Yes Phil, but why?"

"So the shareholders will know what they own and judge how well management is using them."

"Well," she says, flashing that smile which never fails to delight me. "You really have retained an amazing amount of what we covered back in the UK, Phil. But you haven't mentioned the other side of the Balance Sheet. Remember assets are on one side with liabilities or sources of finance on the other."

"Yes of course. I guess that side shows where the money came from to buy the assets, right?"

"Right Phil. I know this may seem pretty obvious now but it's not so straightforward as you might think. I agree with the purposes you've described but there's now a big debate going on about the purpose of these financial statements, partly as a result of the goodwill and brands problems we discussed before the ABT takeover. Many people want the Balance Sheet to do more than show where the money's come from and how the management have used it to buy assets. They want it to value the business and then you're into a whole new ballgame."

She pauses for a moment as Karen comes in with a tray of tea. Karen is now confirmed as my new Secretary and Tracy works for Chris. It was a difficult decision but Karen's experience and long-term commitment to Chapmans was too important to risk losing. And she's been really great – helpful and supportive without any comparisons to Richard with whom she worked so closely. She keeps me in touch with Richard's progress in the UK. Apparently his new venture is getting under way and he's enjoying a new challenge. Effectively his Canadian backers have given him the money to start a new operation in the ready-prepared meals market and have allowed him complete freedom, just what he wants. But he's not once been back to the US and has had very little contact with Barbara – she's already filed for divorce.

As I pour the tea, Chris writes up on the flipchart:

FUNDAMENTAL ACCOUNTING PRINCIPLES

"I'm going to work to the UK conventions Phil because I know them better – I've not really been involved in the detail since I came over here. But there aren't that many differences from the US and I'll mention them where I know them. There are more and more moves to internationalisation of standards these days."

"OK Chris, I'm all ears."

"The first thing to stress is the reason for having accounting principles. It's easy to talk about the purposes of the Profit and Loss and Balance Sheet but much more difficult to apply in practice. How do you calculate what it costs to run a business in a particular year? How do you value assets? You need to use some judgements and you can't always leave it to the management of the company – they may manipulate the methods to suit their own ends. So you need some rules and the first one is probably the most important."

She writes up:

CONSISTENCY

"You mean that every company has to use the same method – surely that's impossible?"

"No Phil, that's not what consistency means in this context. There is some consistency between companies because of the accounting standards which have been developed but there are differences of interpretation between companies and between countries. Each company negotiates with its Auditors its own individual list of accounting policies."

"So what's consistent about that? If they're all doing their own thing, that seems inconsistent to me."

"No Phil, and it's not quite as bad as you make out by the way; there are many similarities. No the whole point of consistency is that, once agreed, those policies are applied consistently by the same company every year, unless there is agreement otherwise."

"And if there is agreement otherwise?"

"Then this must be declared and the impact shown. And there must have been good reasons for making the change."

I'm now having some trouble getting excited about this subject – I have always preferred the practical emphasis of management accounting to the more judgemental issues of financial accounting which tend to make me cynical. I recall the old joke which I heard on a Universal management course years ago. If you ask an accountant what you get when you add two and two, the answer is "What would you like it to be?" I mention this to Chris and she smiles indulgently but is obviously not too pleased about my cynicism.

"OK Chris," I say, "I'll try not to be negative but it's all so abstract. You're usually so good at giving examples. Tell me of an accounting policy at Chapmans where we apply consistency and maybe how we might change it."

"OK Phil. Let's take depreciation as an example. The amounts that we include in our costs each year to write down fixed assets. We've agreed an accounting policy with our auditors to write off assets at various percentages. Plant over ten years, office equipment over five years, computers and cars over three years."

"Are those percentages the same for other companies?"

"Not necessarily. In fact ABT apply different percentages to us and we will have to harmonise at some point. But generally it is logical that there should be differences between companies because some may keep assets longer or wear them out quicker than others. So there'll be a different accounting policy for each company but every one will apply it consistently."

"Unless they decide to change it."

"Unless they agree a change with their Auditors which should arise from a real change in circumstances. For instance, if plant was actually wearing out in seven years, not ten, the policy should be changed and the depreciation period shortened."

"And this should be declared in the accounts?"

"Right and, if it's material, the impact on profit of the change should be shown."

She picks up her pen and writes on the flipchart:

MATERIALITY

"That reminds me of another accounting convention –
materiality," she says. "You only need to show what is
material to the scale of the figures. If it's trivial in relation
to profits, it need not be highlighted."

Again my suspicious and cynical mind makes me think
of those who might take advantage.

"But isn't that wide open Chris?" I say. "Won't people
change the depreciation period to achieve the profits they
want?"

"But that's precisely why the consistency convention is
there Phil. You must be consistent unless you can show
good justification for changing the method. Starting from
the profit figure you want and then deciding on the
accounting convention you need to achieve it is creative
accounting and that's not acceptable practice."

"Now come on Chris. Be realistic. Surely it happens all
the time. I know we've done it at Chapmans, particularly
with stock write-offs and bad debt provisions. We always
load them when we've had a good year and try to provide
less when we need more profit."

She smiles at me, puts down her pen and sits down at
the table.

"This is difficult because I'm speaking from a theoretical
standpoint and you're confirming the reality, that, in
practice, these principles are stretched to the limit by
natural management behaviour and by negotiation. It's
really a question of degree – the accounting policies provide
the framework which limits the abuse to acceptable levels.
And the third accounting principle makes sure that at least
the manipulation is mainly one way."

"And what's that?" I ask.

She turns to the flipchart and writes:

PRUDENCE

"Who's she?" I joke rather weakly and get an
undeserved smile.

"Well, your example of the bad debt provision was a
good one because you will always have more trouble
persuading the Auditors to cut out the bad debt provision

than you will getting them to increase it. Increasing a bad debt provision and thus reducing profit is prudent so the Auditors will be more likely to turn a blind eye to that than to any attempt to make the profit higher. Similarly they'll be happier about a shorter depreciation period than a longer one."

"Is this because accountants are just naturally conservative?" I ask.

"Yes, that is part of their training and with good reason. Their job is to protect the shareholders and avoid profits being overstated. An overstatement could mislead the shareholders into thinking that the management are better than they really are or maybe lead to payment of a dividend which wasn't justified by profits."

"Any other examples of prudence which I can relate to Chapmans?"

She stops to think for a while.

"Yes Phil. You know we usually write off major refurbishments of buildings to repair costs in the Profit and Loss Account. We could take part of the cost to the Balance Sheet and depreciate it, thus increasing profits in the short term. But we've taken the prudent accounting policy."

"Who would have made that decision?"

"I don't know. I guess it goes back years. Probably it's been there ever since Chapmans was formed. That is one problem with the consistency principle – it does encourage companies to stick with their original accounting policies and this may not always be appropriate as they grow and become public."

She stops speaking and looks at her watch.

"It's getting close to 4 o'clock so can we carry on tomorrow?"

"Yes, of course Chris. I'm free after our usual morning meeting. Have we finished general accounting principles because I'd like to move on to ABT's methods? I'm still irritated about Talbot's attitude and I want to know why our profit looks so small under their system."

"And what we can do to improve it I hope," says Chris. "We really have got to start thinking in those terms, because ABT aren't going to change the rules for us. But, to answer your question, yes we've just about finished general principles. There's the 'going concern' concept which I think we've talked about before – the assumption in asset valuations that the business will carry on in existence and that assets will not therefore have to be disposed on a forced sale basis."

"Yes. Wasn't there something in the paper recently about one of these Australian whizz-kids going bust – the Auditors had qualified the accounts by saying that it was not a going concern."

"Right," replies Chris beginning to put on her jacket and turning to the mirror on my wall to tidy her hair. "They were saying that they could not apply the going concern principle because they had doubts about whether the company would carry on in business. Thus they had no choice but to qualify the accounts and tell the shareholders about their reservations."

She picks up the pen again, walks to the flipchart and adds this principle to the list, thus increasing it to show:

CONSISTENCY
MATERIALITY
PRUDENCE
GOING CONCERN

"Right my love," she says, "I must be off. I'll see you tomorrow, or should I say tonight? Are you coming round to my place?"

"Yes, of course Chris, if you'll have me," I say, knowing that wild horses wouldn't drag me away while Jean is in the UK. "I'll be round about 7.30."

"I know I shouldn't do this here," she says and bends down to kiss me full on the lips, holding the back of my head as she does so. I think to myself that this is not the sort of thing the Company President should be doing in his office with his CFO but there's no way I'm going to stop her. I just can't wait till the evening when I can hold this beautiful girl in my arms and forget all about the problems of Chapmans and ABT.

Just then Karen comes in with a piece of paper in her hand and we both quickly break away from our embrace. There are a few seconds of embarrassed silence and I say, "OK Chris, see you after the morning meeting tomorrow," but I know that there's nothing I can do to retrieve the situation. Karen now knows and we both know she knows, though I'm absolutely certain that she will not tell anyone else. But I can tell from the expression on Karen's face that she's not at all pleased at what she's seen and that I am lowered in her estimation. I decide not to say anything about the incident just yet and, after Chris has gone, I ask her about the message.

"It's from North Bergen," says Karen in a formal and abrupt tone, not using my first name as she normally would.

"Steve says that one of the dough mixers has blown out and will be out of action for two weeks."

North Bergen is our pancake and doughnut factory, based in a terribly run down part of New Jersey, just across the Lincoln tunnel from New York. Steve is the Factory Manager, a great character who is one of our best operators. Unlike some of the managers out here, he knows what he's talking about and, if he says it's going to be out of action for two weeks, it will be. And it's a disaster. We only have two high volume mixers and they're both at Bergen. Having one of them out of action is going to cause us severe problems – we're bound to have to restrict output at a time when our customers are likely to be screaming for supplies. It's now mid November, Thanksgiving Day is next week and we will have to cut back on doughnut products – one of our specialities.

How our competitors will enjoy this.

"Tell Steve to come to our morning meeting tomorrow Karen. And ask him to bring the latest costings on all products which go through the mixer. And Karen."

"Yes."

I decide I'd better say something.

"I'm sorry you were embarrassed just now – I would be most grateful if you could try to forget what you saw."

"I can't forget it but I won't tell anyone else if that's

what you're concerned about," she replies with a voice which seems to be faltering with emotion.

"Thanks Karen," I reply, wishing I'd never started this conversation. "I guess I knew that would be the case. I just hate putting you in this position."

Just then the phone rings to rescue us from an embarrassing interchange which I wasn't sure how to end.

Karen picks up the phone.

"OK," she says, "put her through."

She passes me the phone and says, "It's your wife calling from the UK."

Then she walks out and slams the door.

Chapter 12

It's 8.15 next morning and ten of my team are sitting round the table in the Board Room. I've tried to make this room more available for routine meetings since ABT took us over and I've removed the pictures of the Chapman family which used to be there.

As is the tradition, we're all tucking into a working breakfast which is supposed to make these meetings into a product testing session too. This morning the problems at the North Bergen factory make us forget the quality of the food.

The rule is that everyone who is in comes to these meetings and they are a valuable opportunity for us all to keep in touch. Some days there's nothing specific on the agenda and we just chat; other days a number of people come with their own issues to raise. When things are going well these meetings are great fun and make me realise how lucky I am to be running a major US business like Chapmans. Other days, like today for instance, I'm not so sure. There are the threats from Talbot still ringing in my ears, my secretary is only talking to me when she really has to and now we have the problem of the blown out dough mixer.

Steve is describing the technical problems to his boss John Madden, who always makes an excellent contribution to these meetings as VP Production. I switch off and smile across the table to Chris who looks as fantastic as usual, remarkable considering the small amount of sleep I know she had. It suddenly seems bizarre to be sitting here in Chapmans' Board Room with this stunning girl, and all these other people who don't know that, a few hours ago, our naked bodies were entwined together on the king-size bed in her New York apartment. I feel rather smug but then I remember yesterday's telephone conversation with Jean and I'm aware that things aren't so wonderful. I still have a wife and family who I don't want to lose.

Jean rang me to say that she would be a few more days in the UK and I hate myself for feeling pleased about that. Normally I wouldn't have been able to wait for her to come home but this time the delay will mean a few more nights of passion with Chris. I'm rather surprised that Jean wants to stay longer because normally a few days with our parents is more than enough. I think that it would serve me right if she found someone else too but I know she never would. That's what makes me feel so guilty – I know that Jean doesn't deserve a husband who's unfaithful, particularly as she's forgiven me and taken me back before.

Steve finishes his explanation which is the signal for the rest of us to come back into the meeting. I ask Steve for his recommendations about production priority.

"We've got to fulfil existing orders Phil," he says, "then I suggest we focus on pre-packed sixes – you remember they have the highest contribution ratios of all the dough products. After that it's Danish."

I look across at Chris and think that she'll be pleased about the way I've applied her lessons from our days at Lawrensons. I've managed to convince Chapmans' management of the importance of looking at contribution ratios as a way of deciding on the product mix which will maximise profitability. And here is a clear case where we need to make choices. I look down the profitability statement of products from the North Bergen factory which the Factory Cost Accountant produces each month:

	Sale Price per Case	Variable cost	Contribution	%
Pre-packed sixes	9.30	4.93	4.37	47
Danish	6.20	3.84	2.36	38
Apple Donuts	7.00	4.27	2.73	39
Ring Donuts	5.00	3.55	1.45	29
Jelly Donuts	5.80	3.94	1.86	32
Bulk Packs	13.40	9.92	3.48	26

"We'll just have to warn our customers for Bulk Packs," says Henry, "They'll have to take lowest priority. But are we doing everything we can to replace production? Are there any temporary arrangements we can make? We're just going to drive our catering and hotel customers into the arms of our competitors."

While John outlines some possibilities for obtaining temporary extra production from local small suppliers, I notice that Chris gets up to talk to Steve and seems to be asking him a number of questions. Then she comes over to me and whispers, "Phil. Can I just have a few minutes to explain something to the meeting?"

I know from past experience that the glint in her eye means she's on to something and that there's no point in trying to stop her. I bang the table and ask everyone to give Chris their attention. I know that's no problem for the young men present because there's nothing they'd rather do than look at her. I see that Steve, who is a tall, good-looking guy, seems to enjoy the attention she's giving him and I feel an absurd pang of jealousy.

Chris stands by the flipchart at the end of the conference room and writes up some of the figures I see on the report in front of me.

	Contribution	%
Pre-packed sixes	$4.37	47
Bulk Packs	$3.48	26

"Now," says Chris, obviously enjoying the attention and reminding me how she loves an audience when she's helping others to understand management accounting concepts, "Phil has quite rightly taught you to look at contribution percentages in order to determine optimum product mix. I'm a great believer in that, in fact I helped Phil to improve our company's profitability when we were in the UK using this same approach. But the implicit assumption in this approach is that the market is the limiting factor."

"I'm not sure I understand what you mean by that Chris," says Henry, who never was very good with numbers. "Isn't the market always the limiting factor? That's why we need my sales force."

"But it's not going to be for the next two weeks Henry. What will limit our sales is the capacity of the remaining dough mixer to produce the limited volume of products which can go through it. And, in that situation, it is not contribution as a percentage of sales which we should be looking at. We should be working to a ratio which tells us how we can maximise contribution from the limited hours when the dough mixer can operate."

I suddenly understand what she means. Each product will have a different utilisation of time through the machine which will determine how many can be produced during a given period. Those products which use only a small amount of time for each dollar of sales should get priority while there is limited machine capacity, even if they make a lower margin.

Chris carries on almost as if she can read my thoughts. The others don't seem to have understood, as all I see as I look around the table is a row of puzzled faces. I don't know why they all find management accounting, which is usually little more than applied common sense, so difficult. But Chris goes on to explain in a way which, I feel sure, will make it clear to everyone.

"Now let's look at two products which have the highest and lowest profitability in the range – pre-packed sixes and bulk. Steve hasn't got the data with him but he reckons that, because of the specification required for pre-packed, they need to spend roughly twice the time in the mixer compared with bulk. Let's say that, for every $100 of sales pre-packed need six hours on the machine but bulk only need three."

She now writes up:

	$100 of sales	Contribution	Machine Hours	Contribution per hour
Pre-packed sixes	100	47	6	7.8
Bulk Packs	100	26	3	8.7

"So, if these figures are correct – and of course, we'll need to get more accurate timings from Steve's cost accountant – it could be that Bulk are the most profitable product for us to sell while the machine continues to be the limiting factor."

I look at these figures and see clearly how we've been missing opportunities for years because we've never used this approach before. But I have a doubt which I decide to raise.

"I can see what you're saying Chris and I think we can use this idea of relating contributions to constraints in quite a few other contexts, but why have you taken sales value as the basis? Isn't it weight of mix which will be the key factor? You need to put in more mix for the same sales value of bulk compared with pre-packed or at least I should think so."

"Sure Phil. You're right of course," she looks round the room with a smile. "I'm not sure if you guys know how hot your President is at management accounting. Once he gets hold of an idea, it's hard to keep up with him."

"And look who taught me," I say, giving Chris a look which shows more than it should about my feelings for her.

I glance round the room and notice that the others seem to be showing more embarrassment than admiration, and tell myself for the second time in two days that I shouldn't be having an affair with my CFO.

Chris breaks the embarrassed silence by saying, "Anyway, you're right Phil. The costings will need to go down to the level of contribution per ton of mix – I was just using sales value to illustrate the principle of contribution per limiting factor. And, by the way, I think you're right about there being other ways in which it can be applied. I used it a lot when I was with McKenzies and it can transform the way you think about profitability."

"When you think about it Phil," intervenes Jane, now installed as our VP Marketing, "it's no more than our customers, the retailers do. Their constraint is square footage of sales area and they are always quoting contribution per square foot figures when they compare profitability between products. Henry, you mentioned how Valumart were complaining about our pack sizes and that's the reason."

I'm curious about Jane's comment and realise that I don't know enough about how our customers evaluate product profitability. I'm also pretty sure that Henry doesn't either. As VP Sales, he's the one who really ought to know how our customers look at these things.

"What do you mean by contribution Jane?" I ask, "is that the same as their gross margin or do they take off other costs?"

"They take off other costs Phil, like distribution, storage, handling, store overheads. I know because I've just employed a Brand Manager who came from Valumart and I've been amazed by their sophistication."

"Well, can we fix up a meeting about this?" I say. "Henry, you arrange it and I'd like your Brand Manager to be there Jane and you Chris, and me. And anyone else who can contribute."

Henry agrees to do this though I notice his lack of enthusiasm. Henry is great with customers at the interpersonal level but is not very numerate and he shies away from anything which involves complex analysis. For the first time I question whether I've got the right man in this crucial job. Sales is no longer about socialising with customers. It's about preparing the ground for complex negotiations, knowing how some very sophisticated customers make decisions and being able to analyse a wide range of detailed information, including the customer profitability system which I installed about a year ago, based on what Chris and I introduced at Lawrensons. I'm not sure if Henry's up to it and I think that, before too long, I may have to grasp this nettle.

The meeting breaks up and everyone goes their separate ways. Chris remains, looking down at the table, a morose expression on her face. This is something I've never seen before.

I say lightly, "Are you ready for our meeting about ABT's financial systems Chris?"

"Yes Phil," she replies, "I guess so. But I think we've got to talk about other things too – I'm not sure we can go on as we are. I'm certain they all know what's going on between us and I don't think I can cope with it." Her voice is almost tearful now.

"Let's talk in my office," I say and we walk out together. Once again, I am aware that I've managed to turn a blissfully happy life into one hell of a mess.

Chapter 13

There's an awkward silence as we walk together back to my office and I glance sideways to see the tense expression on her face. I think to myself how unpredictable women can be. Since we started our affair, I've been amazed at her apparently relaxed attitude but now I wonder if it was a façade. Or maybe she now knows what I guess I knew deep down from the beginning, that you can't carry on as we are without it sooner or later having an adverse impact on the way we do our jobs.

As we enter my office, Karen looks down at her word processor in a very obvious way – none of the cheery good morning which I normally get from her. This makes it clear to both of us that yesterday has not been forgotten and serves only to reinforce the problem we've created for ourselves.

I pick up the coffee jug which is always ready in my office each morning and pour a cup for both of us.

"OK love," I say, using the term of endearment which I normally only use with Jean, "let's talk. I agree we need to. But I'm not sure I know what we can do about it. Even if we decide to stop our affair, it's not going to change the way we feel about each other – at least I know that's true for me. So what do you want to do?"

She turns her back and looks out of the window, something she does a lot when she needs time to think.

"I don't know Phil," she says, turning towards me with a

resigned expression on her face.

"We've really got two, or maybe three choices Chris."

"Go on then Phil. Spell them out in your usual logical way," she says, trying hard to smile.

"Well, we can stay as we are and live with it."

"And maybe not be as stupid as I was yesterday."

"Well it's not just you Chris – I'm to blame as well. But we will both have to carry on as if we are just work colleagues and that shouldn't be so difficult."

"But it is Phil, you know that. But tell me about the other options."

"You know them really Chris, don't you? Either we end our affair or one of us leaves Chapmans."

"Which would mean me?"

"I don't know love. I just don't know."

"Yes it would Phil, you know that. There's no-one else here that could. Anyway the whole idea is ridiculous."

"How ridiculous is ending our affair?"

"Not ridiculous Phil. Just painful. I really am enjoying our time together though I do feel terrible about Jean and the children. And I'm not sure ..

"Not sure about what Chris?"

Again she gets up and goes to the window. She speaks while still looking outside.

"I guess I'm not sure where it's going Phil. And I'm not sure I want to know."

Then she turns round and smiles very sweetly but rather artificially.

"Phil. Can we get down to work please. We both know that we've got to carry on as we are, at least for the time being. And maybe we need to have a long talk some time outside of this place. In the meantime there'll be no more kisses and no more loving looks while we're at Chapmans. OK Mr Moorley?"

"OK Miss Goodhart," I reply and we smile at each other, knowing that this is something we're going to have to resolve one way or the other. As Chris empties some papers from her briefcase onto my table I think to myself that there is another option we didn't mention and that would be for us to live together, maybe even marry. I wonder if that is in her mind too but she transferred her attention to ABT's financial measurement methods and I try to do the same.

"Now Phil," she says and I notice the change in her voice as she assumes her 'teaching mode' which somehow seems to get the right balance between being instructive but not patronising. "You recall the times at Lawrensons when we discussed management accounting and its different role and purpose compared with financial accounting."

"Yes of course Chris. And I practise it here. I've had quite a few battles with Carl when he told me that information couldn't be produced because it was outside the financial accounting reporting format. I told him that the management team decide on management accounting information and that his job is to produce anything which is useful to us. He finally got the message and all his team eventually began to think in those terms."

"I'm not sure that Carl or the others really have got the message. They produce what you have asked for but they do little else to generate management accounting information pro-actively and that's what they should be doing."

"I know what you mean. But why are you raising the issue of management accounting again? What's this to do with ABT's methods of measuring our performance?"

"Well Phil. Can't you see what they are doing? They are separating their financial information into two parts – the financial accounts for shareholders and management accounts to assess and compare the performance of divisions."

She writes up on the flipchart.

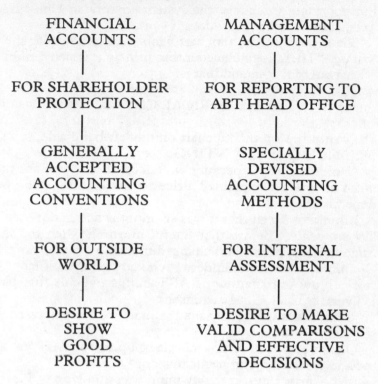

FINANCIAL ACCOUNTS	MANAGEMENT ACCOUNTS
FOR SHAREHOLDER PROTECTION	FOR REPORTING TO ABT HEAD OFFICE
GENERALLY ACCEPTED ACCOUNTING CONVENTIONS	SPECIALLY DEVISED ACCOUNTING METHODS
FOR OUTSIDE WORLD	FOR INTERNAL ASSESSMENT
DESIRE TO SHOW GOOD PROFITS	DESIRE TO MAKE VALID COMPARISONS AND EFFECTIVE DECISIONS

"So you can't really blame ABT for using another system Phil because it's their way of applying management accounting principles."

"And it makes me depressed and demotivated because the profit we used to report has disappeared," I reply, quite irritated by her defence of ABT.

"They might argue that it's to stop you getting complacent and maybe to allow Talbot to compare you with others on a valid basis."

I feel very defensive about this and I'm just about to continue the argument when she laughs out loud at me.

"Phil," she says, "I'm not ABT you know – I didn't invent the system. I'm just trying to explain it."

She's right of course. I get up to pour myself another cup of coffee.

"OK Chris, I'm sorry and also pretty stupid. Because I'm not going to change the system anyway so I might as well get to know it. How does it work?"

She returns to the flipchart again and talks while she's writing. "There is one accounting principle which I didn't cover yesterday Phil and that is:

HISTORICAL COST

She writes this on the flipchart on the left-hand side, under FINANCIAL ACCOUNTING.

"I didn't cover it because we talked about it before the takeover when I explained Price to Book ratio – do you remember?"

I think to myself that it was six months ago and it seems like six years. Before that fateful morning when the fax came from Universal and changed the life of so many of us, Chapmans was independent, relaxed, a happy place to work. Now the shadow of ABT hangs over us just like Universal's used to at Lawrensons.

"Phil," says Chris, "what's the matter? Do you want to stop?"

Once again, I'm letting my hang-up about ABT get to me and I decide that it needs to stop.

"No Chris, I'm sorry. My mind was wandering. Please carry on. And yes of course I remember. You said that, in the UK, companies sometimes revalue fixed assets to a market value basis but, in most countries, the convention is historical cost, however much that cost may be out of date."

"And why do you think that is Phil? What other accounting convention is likely to lead you down that road?"

"Prudence? Because it would not be prudent to assume a profit on fixed assets unless it's actually been realised. Am I right?"

"You are Phil. You see it's a bit like the argument we had about brands – if you allow companies to revalue assets, you're introducing yet another area of judgement and companies might do it for the wrong reasons – to make their Balance Sheet look good and thus impress the bank for instance. At least no-one can argue with historical cost because it's what you actually spent when you bought the asset."

"OK, I understand the reasons though it all seems a bit defeatist. Didn't you once tell me that your MBA tutor said it's better to be approximately right than precisely wrong?"

She laughs, puts down her pen and comes over towards me. But then I see her pause and sit on the side of my desk, still a few feet away.

"Phil," she says, "your memory and use of logic just bowls me over sometimes. That quote was by a Dutch Professor who, in fact, was justifying the sort of system which ABT operate. That is exactly why ABT change the system for management accounting purposes because they're not tied to the accounting conventions used in published accounts."

She then writes up, on the right-hand side of the flipchart under the MANAGEMENT ACCOUNTING column:

REPLACEMENT COST

Then she sits down at the table and looks across at me.

"Now Phil," she says, "forget for a moment your natural emotional reaction to ABT's system. Just use your usual rational approach and think about the impact which historical cost accounting has on the profits of companies, particularly where you want to make comparisons."

My mind wanders back to my days at Universal when I made a good impression at a company course by questioning whether direct comparisons should ever be made when each company has a unique history, environment and market position. I mention this point to Chris.

"I remember discussing it with you at the time Phil and it's a valid point. But the fact remains that ABT and many other companies do make comparisons and, if they do, they are justified in using the most appropriate accounting basis for them. Put yourself in Talbot's place if that's not too painful for you. What would be the impact of using historical cost methods on the Return on Capital comparisons of the companies in the group?"

I look at the flipchart and see again what she has written at the bottom of it.

<table>
<tr><td>DESIRE TO
SHOW GOOD
PROFITS</td><td>DESIRE TO MAKE
VALID COMPARISONS
AND EFFECTIVE DECISIONS</td></tr>
<tr><td>|</td><td>|</td></tr>
<tr><td>HISTORICAL
COST</td><td>REPLACEMENT
COST</td></tr>
</table>

Before I can answer she says, "And think of both the Profit and Loss Account and Balance Sheet Phil. And fixed assets in particular."

I now begin to understand why Chapmans' results look so poor under the ABT system. My initial thought was that it only affected the Balance Sheet because an increase to replacement cost valuation would increase assets but I had forgotten the impact on costs of the extra depreciation.

"I'm with you Chris," I say, "I see why it hits Return on Capital so much – it's the double squeeze isn't it? Replacement cost valuation increases assets and also reduces profits via extra depreciation which makes it very tough to make a decent return."

"Yes Phil but my question was about the impact if you don't do it. If you use historical cost, those companies with old assets and therefore low depreciation in relation to current prices will look profitable and will appear to be doing better than those who have bought assets more recently. ABT try to bring everyone on to the same basis and measure everything at today's prices."

"Even if it demotivates me."

"They would argue that, though it may be demotivating, it might cause you to think again about profit levels and maybe pricing policy. And it could avoid you hanging on to old assets longer than you should."

This latter point interests me and I ask her to explain it further but she says, "Let me show you some figures first and I'll come back to that point again."

She turns round to the flipchart and I think how perfectly formed she really is, the short skirt of her light blue suit revealing rather too much of her legs to help my concentration. There's no need to ogle her I say to myself – she's yours now. Somehow I manage to concentrate on what she's writing on the new page she's turned over:

FIXED ASSET
ESTIMATED LIFE 10 YEARS

Year	Cost	Depreciation	Balance Sheet Value
1	10,000	1,000	9,000
2		1,000	8,000
3		1,000	7,000
4		1,000	6,000
5		1,000	5,000
6		1,000	4,000
7		1,000	3,000
8		1,000	2,000
9		1,000	1,000
10		1,000	–

"I remember you used those figures when we were at Lawrensons," I say, feeling a touch of nostalgia. "When you first told me what depreciation really is."

"Well you'll probably begin to wonder now because I'm going to show you how ABT work out their replacement cost depreciation. What you must remember though Phil is that this is purely management accounting so you need not worry about it balancing. Remember ABT are like Universal used to be – they only control their companies on a one-sided Balance Sheet basis."

This is something I don't need to be reminded of because it's a method I became used to at Universal and applied to Chapmans before ABT took us over. The best way of thinking about capital employed is to look at the assets side of the Balance Sheet because that is what managers can more easily relate to. You judge them by measuring profit as a percentage to assets employed, thus giving them an incentive to maximise profit and minimise assets. Just as I'm thinking this, I see that Chris has torn off the last page of the flipchart and is sticking it on the notice board on my office wall. Then, as if reading my mind, she writes up:

ASSETS EMPLOYED

FIXED ASSETS
+
STOCK
+
DEBTORS
−
CREDITORS
=
ASSETS EMPLOYED

$$\text{RETURN ON CAPITAL \%} = \frac{\text{TRADING PROFIT}}{\text{ASSETS EMPLOYED}}$$

"It's OK Chris," I say, feeling rather offended that she feels the need to go over this, "I've used this definition a lot. Before you came here I got Carl to do quite a lot of analysis of customers' and competitors' accounts and I always told him to use that definition of capital employed. It concentrates on the assets used in operations and excludes things like cash and tax which are financial in nature. It was you who convinced me of that in my Lawrensons' days: 'Trading profit should be related to assets used in trading', you used to say. I can still hear you now. But there's only one thing you've got wrong."

"Oh yes, what's that," she says, perhaps sensing from my tone of voice that I'm pulling her leg.

"We say FIXED ASSETS PLUS INVENTORIES AND RECEIVABLES LESS PAYABLES over here you know. None of this STOCKS, DEBTORS AND CREDITORS business. And it's Earnings from Operations not Trading Profit. You're obviously not quite converted to the ways of we Americans yet."

She laughs and throws her felt pen at me but, again, I sense her holding back from what could have developed into a moment of fun and warmth between us. Could things ever be truly natural between us while we're both working at Chapmans?

"All right Smartass," she says, using a term she'd never have dreamed of using in the UK, "I suppose you want me to call depreciation amortisation too. Well I'm not going to. We'll use British words while the two of us are here. At least I'm glad you've got past the stage of being confused by the different terms – many managers seem to find it impossible to cope."

She now moves to my notice board and starts to write on the flipchart which shows the depreciation example:

Year	Cost		Depreciation	Balance Sheet Value
1	10,000		1,000	9,000
2	11,000	(replacement cost)	~~1,000~~ 1,100	~~8,000~~ 8,800
3			1,000	7,000
4			1,000	6,000
5			1,000	5,000
6			1,000	4,00ʋ
7			1,000	3,000
8			1,000	2,000
9			1,000	1,000
10			1,000	–

"The £11,000 assumes 10% inflation from Year 1 to Year 2 and reflects the cost of buying that machine if it were to be replaced in its second year," she says, "so ABT insist that the depreciation is increased in the same way. So your profits are reduced by £100 from what they would otherwise have been because you have an extra cost of that amount."

"And who decides it is 10%?" I say. "Surely that's a very difficult figure to arrive at because no-one really knows what inflation of machine prices is in any one year. And you never buy quite the same machine anyway, what with technology changes and everything."

"Remember my Dutch Professor Phil. Better to be approximately right than precisely wrong. That's what ABT would argue and they would argue something else too, something which can work in favour of new investment. If you decide to buy a new machine in Year 2, the depreciation will be just the same as if you keep the old one."

"Yes I can see that Chris but the investment still requires cash and we still have to get a capital approval form through the ABT system. But I hadn't appreciated before that there would be no adverse impact on depreciation if you replace assets. That's interesting."

I now look again at the flipchart but something doesn't seem quite right. I'm happy about the £1,100 depreciation but the increase of the £8,000 to £8,800 doesn't seem right. I can't reconcile it to the original cost-less depreciation. I mention this to Chris.

"You're doing what I said you mustn't Phil," she says and, despite the critical words, the way she says them somehow doesn't offend me.

"You're trying to apply conventional accounting. All I've done is index the £8,000 up by 10% too. You can't balance it to the original cost because the original price levels no longer apply. You can reconcile it by saying – 'let's pretend we bought it for £11,000 in the first place'. Let me show you."

She writes up:

Year	Cost	Depreciation	Balance Sheet Value
1	11,000	1,100	9,900
2		1,100	8,800

Still I have problems accepting this adjustment.

"But what about the adjustment for the previous year?" I ask.

"You're right to raise it as an issue Phil and, when they tried to bring in this kind of system for published accounts in the UK in the 1970s, there was a lot of debate about that point. But remember, this is just management accounts and all ABT do is amend the profit and amend the assets employed to re-assess your profitability."

She then writes on the return on capital equation:

$$\text{RETURN ON CAPITAL} = \frac{\text{TRADING PROFIT} - 100}{\text{ASSETS EMPLOYED} + 800}$$

I look at this and begin to see why it is so difficult for Chapmans to appear profitable under the ABT system.

"And you say that this kind of system is fairly common in big companies Chris?"

"Yes Phil. For management accounts anyway. As I mentioned, there was once a trend to do it for published accounts too – Philips in Holland introduced it many years ago – but you rarely see it now. But there is one further thing which ABT do which is more unusual and which has an even bigger impact on Chapmans' profits."

"Go on then – tell me more."

"Well again it makes no sense from a conventional accounting point of view but they continue to charge depreciation after the initial write-off period has expired, even though there is no Balance Sheet value. And they continue to index it."

"You mean that if that machine is kept for eleven years and would now cost £25,000 to replace, they'll charge £2,500 depreciation?"

"Yes Phil, for ever and a day, as long as you keep the asset. So again it gives you the incentive to replace and stops you holding on to clapped out assets to avoid the depreciation which would be charged on a replacement."

I think about this for a while and really begin to see why Chapmans' profits look so low in ABT's eyes. We have lots of food production machinery which was purchased

over twenty years ago and they're now calculating
depreciation on what it would cost to replace it, though
how they can estimate that accurately I just don't know. I
mention this point to Chris.

"They just use arbitrary percentages which represent
average price increases in food machinery Phil. Remember
the saying..."

"I know Chris, your Dutch Professor. Well I think we'd
better start reviewing our capital expenditure budget and
maybe move some money from capacity expansion to
replacement."

"You see it's working already Phil," she says with a
rather complacent smile on her face, "and, in any case, I
have been meaning to discuss the capital spending plans
with John and produce a report for you quite soon so
maybe we can discuss it then. But are you happy – well
maybe not happy – but do you understand the system?"

"Yes, or as much as I need to. Is that all there is to
replacement cost accounting?"

"No Phil, it's a much bigger issue and, as I mentioned,
if it's applied to financial accounting, you have to think
about the double entry questions too. But there is also the
impact on material costs and stock levels because historical
cost information can be misleading in certain industries.
But it's not a major problem in food companies."

"Why not?"

"Because stocks are fairly low and raw materials are not
held for long periods. But in the oil industry, for example,
the UK companies revalue stocks to replacement cost and
calculate profit as the difference between sales and
replacement cost."

I feel that my brain will not take any more of
replacement cost accounting and I decide not to pursue the
complexities of the oil industry and the book entries
involved. But just as I am thinking that it would be nice to
finish all this and look at the morning's post, Chris opens
up yet another page of the flipchart and says:

"And there's one more thing about ABT's system which
I still haven't covered and which has the biggest impact of
all."

"The interest charge you mean."

"Right Phil. Do you know how this works?"

"I think so but some figures to explain it would be helpful."

She consults her papers on my table.

"Right, let's give you the Chapmans figures for the last 12 months, adjusted for the special depreciation method but before the interest charge."

$$\frac{\text{Trading Profit}}{\text{Assets Employed}} \quad \frac{30,621}{272,641} = 11.2\% \quad \text{Return on Capital}$$

"Which used to be over 20% before ABT changed the methods," I say, still sore about the system but gradually coming round to a more positive approach and a determination to do something about it.

"Now," says Chris, "it's a little misleading of Talbot to say we're making a loss because all the calculation is really showing is that we're making less than 12% Return on Capital. Let's see how it works."

TRADING PROFIT BEFORE INTEREST	30,621
12% CHARGE ON ASSETS EMPLOYED (272641)	32,716
	———
NET TRADING PROFIT/(LOSS)	(2,095)

"So why do they do it Chris? Universal didn't work that way."

"Not exactly. But they used to say that, unless you made 10%, you weren't really contributing. This is really the same message in a different way. They will still calculate ROC in the way I've done but they are also showing you that, unless you make 12%, the amount that they regard as the minimum acceptable return, they're not prepared to call it real profit."

"And I suppose they have a point because, before ABT took us over, we'd have had to borrow some of the money to buy those assets and there would have been an interest charge."

"Yes Phil. So maybe ABT's systems aren't so bad after all. I'd much rather we directed our energies into improving profits, now that you fully understand the system."

I know that she's speaking to me in a way which the Company President shouldn't really accept from his Chief Financial Officer, whether or not he's in love with her. But I also know she's right. We're in ABT now and there's no point in being bitter or resentful. The best response to Talbot is to make Chapmans profitable under any system.

"So what's your first profit improvement suggestion Chris?"

"The product and customer profiles Phil. I'm convinced that our costs in all areas are too high because of the fragmentation and complexity of our ranges – too many small uneconomic customers and products."

Just then there's a loud knock on the door. This is most unusual as Karen sometimes comes in during my meetings but she never knocks.

I shout "Come in" and when nothing happens, I walk to the door and open it. Karen is standing there with Carl behind her. Karen, in her own unsubtle way, is showing her disapproval of what she saw yesterday. I also wonder what Carl is making of it.

From the look on Carl's face, I can see that he wants to see me urgently. I beckon him in and try to avoid catching Karen's eye.

"Phil," he says, "I'm sorry to interrupt but the ABT Internal Auditors have suddenly arrived."

"What," says Chris, coming towards us by the door, "but they're not due for three months yet Carl. Surely it's a mistake."

"Apparently it's their management consultancy division Chris. They say they're here to appraise the management policies and practices of the company and they are authorised to see anything and anybody. What shall I do with them?"

I look at Chris and she nods.

"I think you'd better show them in Carl," I say, thinking that maybe Universal weren't too bad to work for after all.

Chapter 14

I'm standing in the arrivals hall of JFK and I'm feeling pretty cheesed off. It's 11.00 am and I've been here four hours, waiting for Jean, Angie and Mark to return from their trip to the UK. The announcement said 'Delay due to adverse weather conditions at Heathrow' and the TV screen has just shown 'landed' so I'm expecting them any time now.

I'm feeling very frustrated when I think of the wasted time. I never have been very good at waiting and, once I'd scanned today's New York Times, I could find very little to do except think. And whenever I think I get depressed.

At Chapmans the Internal Auditors are leaving no stone unturned in their 'management investigation'. I had no idea that Internal Auditors did more than investigate accounting systems – certainly that was their role at Universal in the old days. But these people want to look at everything – product range, customers, costings, discount levels, capital investment projects, marketing plans, the lot.

I contacted Arnold Kaufman at ABT Headquarters because this invasion has almost been the last straw as far as I am concerned. I agreed to support ABT in their bid for Chapmans mainly on the strength of Kaufman's personal assurance that I would have a high level of autonomy – now I see it as so much bullshit. They pay lip service to autonomy but really they're even more controlling than Universal. They say it's because the financial results are poor but I've made discreet enquiries among other company Presidents in the ABT Group.

Only yesterday I chatted on the phone to Earl Hennessy, President of their frozen food company in Pennsylvania. He was cynical about the whole business.

"Oh you've got the KGB in, have you pal, well the best of luck. They produced a hundred page report on my company and Matt Talbot brings it with him every time he comes."

"Am I right that it's only those who are producing poor financial results who get this kind of interference?" I asked.

"No Phil. It's just Kaufman and his henchmen. They're like that. They just like kicking ass – they've got nothing else to do. But I'll tell you one thing."

"Yes?" I asked, feeling that I wasn't going to like the answer.

"The staff in his Audit Department may be tough and demanding but they're very sharp. If you can forget who they work for, they're likely to give you good value."

This comment interested me, because it reflected precisely what Chris has been saying to me ever since they came. She says they are accomplishing in days some of the things she has been wanting to start over the last few months but hasn't had the time or resources to start. The only problem for me is that it's bound to be seen as a reflection on my management of Chapmans that there is so much room for improvement. Anyway the Auditors are due to present the first stage of their findings this afternoon but it now looks as if I'll miss the lunch meeting I was going to have with Chris beforehand.

Just then I see the three of them coming through the arrival gate. Jean's wearing a pink tracksuit and is looking as happy and as well as I've seen her for ages. I'm surprised because visiting parents and parents-in-law is usually a strain. The kids look fine. Mark now almost as tall as me with his hair tending to grow long, following the trend of his American friends. Angie now a mature seventeen year old, a real beauty with her mother's eyes and a figure which turns heads as she runs towards me ahead of the other two.

Angie gives me a hug and I say hi to Mark – I've never been sure how to greet him. Shaking hands is too formal and we still have enough of our English reserve to hold back from hugging and kissing like they do over here. I've missed the kids so much, and feel yet more guilt about the fact that I was almost wishing they could stay away longer as I lay in bed with Chris last night.

I kiss Jean full on the lips and we smile at each other in a way which others (including the kids, I hope) would see as just as loving as it's been ever since we got together again. But I know it's not and so I suspect does she. Yet still she looks happy and radiant and can't stop chattering about what happened in England as we drive along the expressway, away from the airport. She even makes no complaint when I say that I'll have to get right back to the office after I've dropped them off at home.

I manage to make it back to the presentation which is starting at 2.30pm and I even get a chance to have a quick chat with Chris first.

"They've focused on our product and customer ranges first Phil," she says as we walk towards the Board Room. "They've looked at some of our costs in relation to other ABT companies and they've also compared the number of customers and products with other similar size operations. They believe that the profile of customers and products is an important driver of cost levels because of the complexity it creates. You remember I've mentioned this to you before."

"Yes I know Chris but it's all very theoretical. They'd better come up with some ideas to reduce the range in a way which improves profit. It's alright saying we have lots of small products and small customers but what do you do about it?"

"I think you might be surprised Phil."

Then, stopping before the door, she says, "and Phil, please will you do something for me?"

"Yes," I say, looking straight into her blue eyes and knowing that I'd do practically anything.

"Please have an open mind and don't be defensive or negative. These people are only doing their job and I think they have a lot to offer."

I try very hard to do what she says and certainly the two Chief Auditors who are making the presentation are decent enough fellows. I guess they're used to people like me being defensive and, from the moment they arrived, they tried to establish good relationships with all my management team. But pathetic though I know it is, I can't help being jealous about the way that Chris and the man who seems to be in charge, Bob Palmer, have got on from the moment he entered the door. My inferiority complex where Chris is concerned made me notice that he is the complete opposite to me in many ways – young, tall, strikingly good looking with thick blond hair, exactly the same shade as hers.

When they're together, they look like a couple of characters from Dallas and I can't help hating him and wondering how long my affair with this gorgeous girl can go on when there are men like him around.

Palmer has an overhead projector set up and we all sit back to hear what he has to say. He shows that he is a skilled presenter by introducing himself and setting the background very effectively. He talks about the role of the Audit Department, how they are here to help and how their recommendations do not necessarily imply that we are inefficient.

"Every company in the Group has room for continuous improvement," says Palmer, "and we can be the catalysts which start you on the road to higher profitability."

"I would like to thank every one for their cooperation, particularly Chris, Jane and Henry," he continues, though I notice that his eyes go to Chris and not the other two. "This first phase has needed a lot of information about product and customer ranges and I'm most grateful for your efforts. I would like now to hand over to Steve who is going to start this presentation with some cost comparisons with other ABT food companies."

Steve is about the same age as his colleague but a different sort of man altogether. Small, bespectacled, studious looking, like the classic American college boy who never made the football team. Yet he has a certain dynamism which comes through when he speaks and Chris has already told me that he is the brains behind the work they're doing.

After a short preamble, Steve shows some cost comparisons which catch my attention. But they also arouse the defensive reactions which Chris warned me against but which have never been far short of the surface since we became part of ABT.

The overhead transparency says:

ABT FOOD COMPANIES

EXPENSES AS A PERCENTAGE OF SALES	Chapmans	Langans	Werners	Naylors
Production	12.7	11.2	12.1	10.6
Warehousing & Distribution	7.2	6.4	7.2	7.0
Selling	5.8	4.1	4.3	5.0
Marketing	2.8	2.6	3.1	2.4
Research	2.4	2.2	2.1	1.7
Product Development	2.6	2.5	2.0	1.9
Administration	5.7	4.9	5.3	6.0

"We believe that costs as a percentage of sales are key factors in long-term success and they should always be looked at as part of strategic decision making," says Steve.

I'm just going to interrupt and say that many of these comparisons are unfair and illogical when Chris jumps in first. I suspect that she knew I was going to comment and is trying to pre-empt me.

"Steve," she says, "I think you should make it clear to everyone, as you did to me yesterday, that many of these comparisons are influenced by the different size and nature of the other operations, compared with Chapmans."

"Yes Chris, you're right," replies Steve and I begin to suspect that this may be a rehearsed double act, "but the pattern is so consistent that at least it provides a justification for investigating further. That's all we're trying to do by this kind of analysis – we're looking for initial evidence that Chapmans' costs may be higher than the norm. And we can also support this by analysis of competitors who are not in ABT though we do not have access to quite so much detailed cost data."

I want to back up Chris's point by saying that none of these companies are anything like Chapmans. Langans are into far more chilled products than us, Werners are based in Chicago and have a vastly different distribution pattern, Naylors subcontract much of their production and share R & D facilities with another ABT company. But by now Steve is on to the comparisons with competitors and I'm disturbed by the figures.

	Chapmans	Ballards	Kotter
Research & Development	5.0	3.6	2.7
Selling Marketing and Distribution	15.8	13.4	14.2
Administration	5.7	6.1	4.1

"I'm sorry Steve," I say, before Chris can get in first again. "I was willing to let the first lot go because of your comment in response to Chris's question. And at least within ABT you have access to full cost details and can check cost classifications. But frankly the comparisons with Ballards and Kotters are worthless. How do you know if they classify costs in the same way as us? I've done a few comparisons of this kind myself and I know that, what we call administration, they may call selling and vice versa. For instance we always put bad debts into selling to encourage the sales managers to take responsibility for them, but some other companies put them in to administration."

"I know Phil," says Steve, a little patronisingly I think to myself. "But you can't escape the evidence of the bottom line."

He then replaces the transparency with another which shows:

	Chapmans	Ballards	Kotter
% Earnings from Operations to Sales	8.8%	11.6%	10.4%

I look across at Chris and try to convey my puzzlement at the 8.8% figure which seems far higher than we have been quoting to Matt Talbot recently. She whispers something across which I can't quite hear and I notice that Steve is now looking at me, waiting for us to give him back our attention. I think to myself that this man is quite an operator.

"Would you like me to explain the figures Phil?" he asks innocently. "I appreciate that they will be different from the internal information you produce for ABT because I've tried to use published accounting information. Thus I've added back the adjustments for replacement cost depreciation so the 8.8% is what you would have declared for the latest half year if you had still been an independent quoted company."

"That's the half year to 30th June?"

"Yes. The other two companies have the same year end so there are no distortions of that kind."

I look across at Chris.

"Chris," I ask, "could you just remind us what that 8.8% would be with the replacement cost adjustment taken off and also how it compares with the same period last year."

It rather surprises me that Chris doesn't respond immediately in her usual way but starts to delve among some papers in the file in front of her. Before she can do so, Bob Palmer intervenes.

"The margin reported to ABT for this half year after adjustment for replacement cost depreciation was 5.4% and the half year figure in your published accounts last year was also 8.8%, though you improved to 9.8% for the full year because of the higher volume in the second half."

I remember that 9.8% figure vividly from our last full year's published accounts – just over $66 million on sales of 678 million. I remember being annoyed at not making the 10%, particularly as the two competitors quoted by Steve both exceeded it even more comfortably than they have this half year.

I glance again towards Chris and see a furious expression on her face as she looks away from me. I guess she's annoyed because I put her on the spot with a question which she couldn't answer but Palmer could. I remember that, despite her apparently easy-going nature and our rather special relationship, she can still be easily upset. I try to catch her eye but again she looks away. I decide I'd better see her afterwards to make the peace – something which I probably wouldn't be doing if I didn't need her favour for other reasons. Again I am acutely aware of the problems of mixing my business and emotional lives.

In the meantime, Steve is continuing with his presentation and the numbers which next appear on the screen grasp my attention in a big way. Steve has moved from more general cost comparisons to the specific issues in Chapmans.

"We note in Chapmans a high degree of management and administrative complexity compared with other companies of similar size which we have investigated. And we put it down, to some extent, to the fragmentation of your product and customer ranges. You really do have the classic 80/20 syndrome as you can see here."

Steve points to the screen which shows the following figures:

VOLUME RANGE PER ANNUM (THOUSANDS OF CASES)	NUMBER OF PRODUCTS	TOTAL VOLUME (THOUSANDS OF CASES)
OVER 5000	1	6,211
2000 – 5000	3	10,273
1000 – 2000	7	13,681
500 – 1000	13	9,495
250 – 500	22	8,490
100 – 250	38	5,278
50 – 100	56	3,996
UNDER 50	78	2,366
TOTAL	218	59,790

I notice that Henry is looking at the figures in the same way as he looks at all numbers which are presented before him – with a pained and puzzled expression.

"What did you mean when you said the 80/20 syndrome?" he asks, rather belligerently. "I've heard the phrase but I'm not quite sure what it means."

I'm staggered by this because Chris has recently explained the term at management meetings, admittedly in other contexts, and I'm sure Henry was there.

"I'm glad you've asked that question Henry, because, as you'll see later, it's even more dramatic when we come to the customer profile," says Steve, "but let me explain using these figures. Remember the left-hand column shows the fairly arbitrary bands we've created to classify products by volume sold per annum. So there are 78 products which sell less than 50,000 cases per annum."

I think that, despite his wimpish appearance, Steve is really the more impressive of the two. He has a certainty and an enthusiasm which come through to his audience – the sure sign of a good communicator.

"Let's have a look at the volume produced by the smallest 80% of your products Henry. Eighty per cent of 218 – the total number of products you produce – is about 174. So if we add the bottom three bands ..."

He points to the screen and writes the totals of the bottom three bands on the transparency.

250 – 500	22		8,490
100 – 250	38		5,278
50 – 100	56	} 172	3,996 } 11,640
UNDER 50	78		2,366
TOTAL	218		59,790

"....we get a total of 172 products – near enough 80% – which produce only ....11,640 thousand cases out of your total volume of 59,790 which is" – he works it out on his pocket calculator – "19.47%."

Jane is now looking interested and maybe a little

defensive. I can see she's going to intervene.

"Now just a moment you guys," she says, "this all depends on how you define a product. We have nowhere near 218 – a lot of those are just variations of pack size or flavour."

"Yes that's true Jane," says Steve, "but we've tried to be consistent in our search for factors which cause complexity and fragmentation and therefore drive costs.

"The test is, does it require a special production run and does it need a separate formulation and costing? If the answer is yes to both those questions, we've included it. So yes, many of your small products are variations of a generic product group but, in our view, your high cost levels are, to some extent, caused by this excessive number of variations."

I can see Jane's hackles rising even further but I notice that Chris nudges and whispers to her and she holds back from what she was going to say. Again I notice how Chris is working in support of these two men from outside and I'm not sure I like it.

I can understand why Jane is feeling defensive because Chris and I have often tried to restrain her from going for more volume by producing small variations on a general theme. Frequently all they do is take away sales from existing products and you end up with the same sales levels but higher complexity. What these people have done is to show me how this tendency has led to the 80/20 position, something which our management information system has never done before.

John Madden now joins in the discussion from his production point of view and repeats a complaint he's made at countless morning meetings. He's obviously grateful for the evidence which this new analysis is now showing.

"I'd like to back up Steve's point," he says. "It doesn't matter how small the change in formulation is, it still requires down time for cleaning and re-mixing. I've often thought that we must be losing money on a lot of these small products if ever it could be worked out."

Steve looks at Bob, his colleague, in what seems to me a

rather smug and self-satisfied way. I begin to think that, though these people's analysis work may be useful, they need to be kept in check.

Steve replies to John. "You'll see our profitability analysis shortly and I think it might surprise many of you. Though maybe not you John because you, more than anybody, know the cost of complexity at first hand."

I decide that, though I agree with a lot of what they're saying, I'd better intervene to give Jane, who is looking increasingly under pressure, a bit of support.

"That's fine gentlemen," I say, trying to summon up the assertiveness which I feel a Company President should show in his own Board Room, "but let's get one thing straight. Financial evaluations are all very well but this is a marketing oriented company and Jane and I base our new product decisions on what our customers require."

I'm pleased to see that Steve is beginning to sweat a little and then Chris comes in too, apparently supporting my point.

"As CFO I'd like to support that but, as Phil would agree I know, it is always useful to back up marketing decisions with a full evaluation of the financial implications. Thus it will very interesting for Jane and Phil to see the bottom line," – I notice how she emphasises those words – "so that in future they will be more aware of the impact of a fragmented product range when they make further decisions of this kind."

Her voice takes on a steely tone towards the end and, as she finishes speaking, she turns back towards Steve and Bob in an exaggerated way which seems to say – let these guys get on with it. I also notice with irritation that both Bob and Steve give her a grateful smile. All is still not well between my CFO and me. It's the first time there's been any significant tension between us since she started at Chapmans and it's even worse that it's happening in public. I can't help worrying how it will affect our personal relationship, particularly as I'm likely to be seeing less of her following Jean's return. I also can't help worrying how wrong it is for me to be feeling this way.

As my mind returns to the issue of Chapmans' product

profile, I see that Steve has moved on to the question of profitability.

"We've tried to allocate fixed costs on the best possible basis and we've tried to be more sophisticated than is normal in these exercises. We've isolated certain costs which are driven by the introduction of new products and by the number of products in existence."

"Which are those?" says a voice on my left and I'm quite surprised that it's Al Morton my VP Personnel, who rarely says anything on these occasions. I'm impressed by the fact that he seems to be taking a keen interest.

Steve, who seems to have a prepared answer to every question, produces a new visual for the OHP. It says:

COSTS DRIVEN BY NEW PRODUCT INTRODUCTIONS

- PRODUCTION
- WAREHOUSING
- DISTRIBUTION
- MARKETING
- RESEARCH
- PRODUCT DEVELOPMENT
- ADMINISTRATION
- INTEREST ON STOCKHOLDING

Steve then spends ten minutes describing how every one of these cost headings is increased when new products are introduced. Not necessarily immediately but certainly in the long term.

How production overheads are driven by the machine set-up time and the cleaning costs each time a recipe mix has to be changed. And how these activities all require extra supervision time. How warehousing costs are influenced because each product has its own space and its own stock record. How distribution costs are driven because vans stack products separately and take lower loads where there are many product variations. How marketing management's time is influenced by the number of products they have to price, promote and review (I notice that Jane nods at this one and I wonder if maybe she's beginning to come round). How 40% of research and development department's time is spent on minor variations to existing products, most of them producing small volume. How invoicing and costing departments' work is directly influenced by the size of the product range. And finally how stock levels are strongly related to the number of SKUs (Stock Keeping Units) which are required to be held.

Steve puts over these points brilliantly and I notice that he seems to have his audience spellbound, with one exception. I see that Henry is looking at his diary, clearly bored out of his mind, and my doubts about him grow. I can't believe that he is so naïve as not to see the implications of this kind of analysis for his own function, particularly after Steve mentioned that the customer profile has an even stronger 80/20 pattern than the product range.

Again I'm impressed that Al Morton leads the questioning. I remember now that Chris recently told me he is doing a part-time MBA at Columbia University.

"So you've based the allocation of those fixed costs you've described on the number of products rather than volume sold?"

"Yes that's right Al," replies Steve, "and the other fixed costs which aren't driven by the size of the range we've allocated on a more general basis. Not always volume – some are based on space taken up in production, some on personnel employed, depending on the nature of the cost. And some costs we can accurately charge to products – like specific promotional or advertising expenditure."

I think that we're getting too bogged down in the mechanics of their calculations so I decide to intervene.

"We'd like to see the results of your calculations Steve. And what you propose we do about them. I must say I have a few concerns about the accuracy and the usefulness of all this complex cost allocation."

"I hear what you say Phil," says Steve, a phrase which they're always using over here and which I find most irritating, "and we'll come to the actions you might take later. My job is to get you to think about long-term profitability and, however difficult and arguable, cost allocations do help to concentrate the mind. Let me show you the profit position and I think you'll see what I mean."

He produces another visual from his pile. The results are quite startling.

	Products selling under 50,000 cases per annum	Products selling 50,000 - 100,000 cases per annum	Products selling 100,000 - 250,000 cases per annum	Products selling 250,000 - 500,000 cases per annum
Number of products	78	56	38	22
Volume (000 cases)	2,366	3,996	5,278	8,490
Turnover ($000)	14,982	24,661	31,626	46,928
Contribution (1)*	7,444	9,616	11,701	16,893
Fixed expenses driven by number of products	(13,467)	(9,660)	(5,582)	(3,239)
Contribution (2)*	(6,023)	(44)	6,119	13,654
Fixed expenses driven by other factors	(3,418)	(5,686)	(6,964)	(9,388)
Net Profit	(9,441)	(5,730)	(845)	4,266

*Contribution (1) is after variable costs only

I look round the room and see that everyone, even including Henry this time, is showing the same reaction as I feel – pure amazement. Again Al is the first to make the point that is on everyone's mind.

"You mean we're actually losing money on all those products where we sell under 250,000 cases a year?"

"Yes," replies Steve, "and remember that's over 80% of the total product range. Though I must make some reservations about the cost allocations before anyone else does. I'm not necessarily saying that in the short term we could save those costs so we have to think very carefully about the implications for action. This calculation is telling you that over the long term, yes, you're losing money because of the implications for your cost structure of all that complexity and fragmentation. Look at the percentage of costs to sales on products under 50,000 cases for instance. If you take the two categories of fixed expenses – costs driven by number of products 13,467 and others 3,418 – you've got costs which are more than 100% of sales. So it's no wonder that your overall cost ratios are high compared with other companies."

Again I notice that Jane is bristling and I'm not surprised. This is a direct indictment of the policies she has been advocating – policies which I should have questioned more closely. It's easy to say yes to each new product proposal because, on its own, each one makes little difference. But this evaluation is showing the long-term consequence of a whole series of decisions of this kind.

Despite the fact that it may be a further condemnation of Jane's policy and my acceptance of it, I ask a question to which I fear I know the answer.

"Steve," I say, "have you got any data on how the 80/20 position has changed over the last few years?"

I thought that this one might stump him but this man is good. Not only has he got an answer, he's got a visual which shows the problem diagrammatically.

"Yes, of course Phil," he says, "that's one of the most interesting aspects and I can illustrate it best by a Pareto graph."

"A what?" says Henry.

"Pareto," replies Steve, "P-A-R-E-T-O. He's the man who gave his name to 80/20 analysis – John here will tell you of its use in quality control measurement. The Pareto graph helps you to see the problem visually and also to measure trends over a period. I've gone back three years to answer your question Phil. But first let me show you the Pareto graph of the product profile I showed you earlier."

He puts a new visual up on the screen.

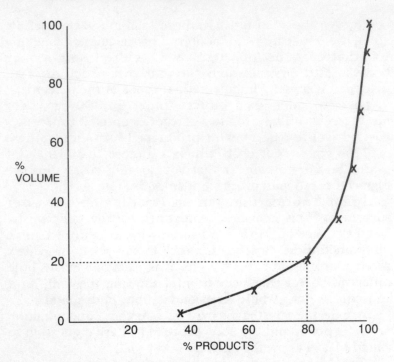

Steve explains, "This converts the product range I showed you earlier into cumulative percentages and then into this diagrammatic form. It can really bring it home to people, particularly those who don't like figures, and also help make the sort of comparison you want to see Phil."

He then shows how the graph works. He says that products under 50,000 cases – 78 of them – are 36% of the total range of 218 but they only produce 2,366 thousand cases out of 59,790 which is 4% of total volume. Thus his first point on the graph is 4% volume 36% products. Then he writes on the flipchart:

	Products	Volume
Under 50,000 cases	78	2,366
50 – 100,000 cases	56	3,996
	134	6,362
% of total	61.5%	10.6%

Then he points to these as the second points on the graph and reminds us that the third point is the same as he had worked out for us earlier, showing the 80/20 effect in practice. He also points out the dotted lines which take the points back to the axes of the graph and confirm the reality of the 80/20 position.

"Now Phil, from the way you asked your question, I don't think you'll be surprised to see this. He overlays another curve on top of the existing one:

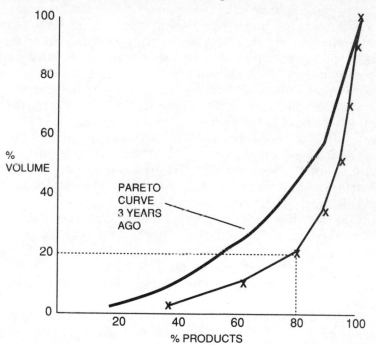

"Note that the curve will always go to the top right-hand corner because 100% of products must always obviously make 100% of volume. But notice that the curve of 3 years ago starts much further to the left because there were far fewer products under 50,000 cases. In fact there were about 17% and they produced about the same volume – 4% as your 36% now do. You'll also see that there was no obvious 80/20 syndrome then – if you read the curve off at 80% products, it's over 40% of volume. And I should also mention that this is more the pattern of curve which we generally expect to see in your kind of business."

I feel the time has come to put these boys on the spot. They are good but they are like many management consultants – all clever calculations and frameworks but limited value when it comes to practical action.

"OK Steve," I reply, "now I hear what you say." I emphasise the 'I' and the 'you' so he will understand that I'm not too happy with the sort of patronising cliché which people accept too easily over here.

"Now Chris may have told you that, though I'm a sales and marketing man by background, I'm also very committed to management accounting evaluations of this kind, mainly because Chris has shown me their value." I think that a little flattery will not come amiss in view of the cold looks I've been getting from her. "And I must say I'm impressed with what you've done so far. But we need to discuss at some point what we do with it because profits are not going to be helped by us all sitting here, being impressed by you, Bob and your Pareto curves. So let's have another look at that P & L evaluation you did because I'd like to hear more about your cost allocations and consider the options open to us."

Chris chips in and I'm pleased that she's being supportive, genuinely this time I think. She says, "I know what Phil's getting at Steve and I'm sure you do. Those costs you mentioned are, in the long term, driven by the size of the product range but it doesn't mean they're easily avoidable."

I note Chris's use of the term avoidable and remember when she used it before. Back at Lawrensons we evaluated the possible sub-contracting of the canteen operation and the evaluation focused on those costs which were avoidable – they could actually be saved as a result of closure. And Chris is making the same point now, using this concept of avoidable cost to reinforce my insistence that we must approach the problem practically. There is no point in getting rid of all products under 50,000 cases if we are not to save costs. All we would do then is lose contribution and be worse off.

As Steve searches among the visuals to find the profit evaluation, I look round the table at those present. John Madden looks happy and relaxed, content that people are at last discussing the production cost problems of a fragmented product range. Al Morton, young, keen, interested, impressing me at this meeting in a way which gives me new ideas about his long-term potential. Chris, looking completely gorgeous as usual – her blonde hair even more curly and tousled then normal, a contrast to the businesslike efficiency of her smart grey suit and the confident manner which radiates authority and presence.

Then there are Jane and Henry who worry me. Jane because, unusually for her, she looks upset and depressed at the implied criticism of her attempts to generate volume from new products. Though I'm convinced of her calibre and long-term potential as a marketeer, I must keep a closer watch on her in future and encourage her to see the financial implications of her decisions.

As I look at Henry making an even more careful study of his diary, I think that, in his case, I may have made the wrong decision by promoting him to VP. The modern sales role requires more than an ability to motivate salesmen and a pleasant manner with clients. It requires a broad business awareness and an interest in levels of profitability as well as sales volume. I knew that Henry had limitations in this area when I promoted him and believed that Chris and I could help him to grow beyond his limited horizons. But he doesn't seem to want to learn. And this afternoon's performance has brought together a lot of doubts about him which give me deep concern about his future with Chapmans.

Steve now re-introduces the visual containing his profitability evaluation and I notice how cleverly he takes my point and uses it, almost giving the impression that he is the one making the reservations about the extent to which the costs are avoidable.

	Products selling under 50,000 cases per annum	Products selling 50,000 - 100,000 cases per annum	Products selling 100,000 - 250,000 cases per annum	Products selling 250,000 - 500,000 cases per annum
Number of products	78	56	38	22
Volume (000 cases)	2,366	3,996	5,278	8,490
Turnover ($000)	14,982	24,661	31,626	46,928
Contribution (1)*	7,444	9,616	11,701	16,893
Fixed expenses driven by number of products	(13,467)	(9,660)	(5,582)	(3,239)
Contribution (2)*	(6,023)	(44)	6,119	13,654
Fixed expenses driven by other factors	(3,418)	(5,686)	(6,964)	(9,388)
Net Profit	(9,441)	(5,730)	(845)	4,266

*Contribution (1) is after variable costs only

"Now let's have a further look at the implications of this for action. As Phil says, the key question is whether the fixed costs are avoidable, either short or long term. Before we examine this however, we should consider the possible ways in which we could improve overall company profitability as a result of this evaluation. And I would state quite firmly that, even if it were desirable from a marketing point of view, we should not just cut out all small products under 100,000 or 250,000 cases per annum and do nothing else."

"Why not?" asks John Madden, perhaps concerned that the benefits to production operations which he was hoping for may be lost.

"Because, unless there is a planned approach to bringing down cost levels, you will just lose the contribution you are now making. Even products under 50,000 cases make 7.444 million dollars contribution after variable costs and that will be lost if we discontinue. The key question then is whether the fixed costs which we have attributed to these products can be made to be avoidable and whether there will be other savings because of lower volume. And that's up to you guys, particularly you John."

"How come?" asks John, looking even more anxious.

"Because most of those costs are in production, warehousing, distribution and development, costs within your control. So if Phil and Jane can be convinced that certain products can be discontinued on marketing grounds, you've then got to prepare a cost reduction plan to convert our allocations into real savings. And I think you can and we'll leave some indications of how we think it can be achieved before we finish our time here. Chris and I have already prepared a provisional avoidable cost schedule which will also include some marketing and admin costs too."

"And perhaps I could also mention the potential impact on interest costs and Return on Capital which you all know are vital at ABT," intervenes Bob Palmer. "I see good potential stock savings if we can rationalise the product range so that will also be part of our evaluation."

"But the first stage must be for Jane and me to get together to decide what is possible from a marketing point of view," I say. "You guys have given us a lot to think about and I'm grateful but there are a lot of issues which we need to think about from the customer's angle."

Steve then comes in with a contribution which makes me appreciate the value of an outside view on these issues.

"But it's not only unravelling the past that is involved here Phil. I accept that it may be difficult to change new product decisions already made. But our evaluation has given you a very good indication of the long-term breakeven point for future new product decisions."

I notice that Jane is looking interested in this point and that Chris again leans towards her with an encouraging word in her ear.

"Oh I see," says Jane, "you're saying that we should only take on new products in future if we're convinced that a certain potential volume level is possible."

"Yes Jane," says Steve, referring again to the profitability evaluation, "we're saying that anything under 100,000 cases per annum is, in the long term, likely to be unprofitable and, though we're less sure about this and you may want to do more precise evaluations, you probably need 250;000 cases to achieve breakeven over all costs. So our recommendation is that this should be your test of long-term potential for new products before you make your decision, unless there are strong marketing reasons for going ahead."

Al Morton is studying the screen intently and makes another intervention. I wonder if maybe he's just doing the financial part of his MBA right now and he's trying to impress us.

"Steve, maybe I'm missing something here but isn't it also to do with price? Surely any new product can be profitable if the price is high enough. Couldn't Jane still go ahead if the price is high enough to cover costs?"

"That's a valuable point Al and will be even more relevant when we look at Henry's customer profile. But I've been assuming in most cases that pricing is constrained by market factors, am I right Jane?" She nods in agreement. "But you may have noticed that the average contribution margins after variable costs are already higher for the smaller products than the average. Under 50,000 cases it is 7,444 on 14,982 which is nearly 50% and the margins get lower as the volume gets higher. For 250–500,000 cases it's 16,893 on 46,928 which is nearly 36% and that's about the company average isn't it Jane?" She nods again and, as she smiles pleasantly at Steve, I see that she's been won over. "So this would indicate that Jane has already been pricing the very small products fairly high and the margins you would need to cover the costs for those below 50,000 cases would just be ridiculous."

"But Al has stimulated a thought in my mind Steve," says Jane. "Pricing could be a way of getting rid of some of the low volume products. It could be easier to price so high that there's just no demand than to tell customers that we are refusing to produce it any more."

"Well," says Bob Palmer resuming control from Steve at the right time, "that's all we try to do with this kind of evaluation – stimulate thoughts and ideas which will enable you to take action to improve profitability in the long term. And thanks to all of you for your valuable contributions." He pauses to look at his watch. "I see it's nearly 4.00 pm and we wish to move on to discuss the customer profile. Should we have a break first? I really think you're going to be even more surprised by these results."

He looks towards where Henry is sitting and then looks back at me, appearing rather embarrassed. I also see Jane suppressing a smile and whispering to Chris. I then turn towards Henry and see the source of their amusement. Henry is fast asleep with his head drooped forward, nodding in time to his breathing.

My view of managing people is that you give them support and you persevere while there is still hope that they will come good. But if there is no hope, they have to go with as much generosity and dignity as possible. And at this moment I decide that, sooner rather than later, Henry has to go.

Chapter 15

I'm in my office with Al Morton, going through a pile of job application forms, trying to decide which of the candidates should go forward to the final shortlist for Henry's old job. Six weeks have now passed since the Internal Auditors' presentation when I decided that I needed a new VP Sales. The Auditors have come and gone and so has Christmas. Things seem to have turned the corner at Chapmans and the business is now going very well. We already have an action plan in place to rationalise the product range and a parallel programme to reduce costs over the next six months. The pre-Christmas sales volume was a record and profits exceeded expectations to take our margin for the year over the forecast we made to ABT in October.

Even the difficult decision I had to make about Henry has had its positive side. It has seemed to galvanise my other VPs into action because they now understand that being a VP at Chapmans does not necessarily mean a guaranteed job for life. And, on the sales side, the impact on morale has been small – Al Morton had done a good job explaining the reasons to Henry's management team. He reported to me that there have for some time been reservations about Henry among the younger and more progressive people in the Sales Function.

Henry left with a very generous settlement only a week after that memorable day when he fell asleep during the

presentation. In fact it was not just that which convinced
me of the need to replace him. It was his attitude later that
same afternoon, when there was a further presentation of
their analysis of Chapmans' customer profile. Henry was
certainly awake when that visual came up on the screen but
his negative and defensive attitude far exceeded anything
that Jane had produced earlier and embarrassed everyone
present. Indeed I came to the conclusion that his general
behaviour was due to a weakness which we all knew he
possessed but which has never been such a problem before
– a tendency to drink too much over lunchtime
entertaining.

The figures were quite startling and, as I later found out
from young Jim Hooker who has taken over Henry's duties
until we find an external replacement, largely a result of
Henry's tendency to take on any new business, however
small and uneconomic. The profile of customers made the
equivalent numbers for products look much less of a
problem by comparison:

VOLUME RANGE PER ANNUM (THOUSANDS OF CASES)	NUMBER OF CUSTOMERS	TOTAL VOLUME (THOUSANDS OF CASES)
OVER 5,000	21	12,352
2,000 – 5,000	30	9,492
1,000 – 2,000	43	6,366
500 – 1,000	76	5,996
250 – 500	164	7,415
100 – 250	712	10,608
50 – 100	629	3,889
UNDER 50	983	3,672
TOTAL	2,658	59,790

Steve emphasised this by another Pareto chart which
confirmed the even more dramatic curve and then made a

comparison with five years ago which just happened to be when Henry took the top position on the sales side.

"Here we have an even more obvious example of the 80/20 syndrome," said Steve, "though I accept that the state of the retail trade is such that all companies have experienced a polarisation between small and large customers. But this is the most dramatic we have ever seen in the food business. And we believe that it's a significant factor in causing your selling expenses percentage to be higher than other ABT companies. Remember I showed you earlier that it was 5.8% of sales and, though we do not have fully detailed data on your competition, our estimate is that you are at least 1% higher than all your top five competitors."

Again I saw how useful it can be to have the outside view. Chris could have organised such an analysis but would not have had the same information or the same credibility when presenting its significance. We might have dismissed such a profile as being part of the inevitable trend towards fewer, bigger retail customers with the consequence that there will also be a long tail of small customers to serve – those small retailers outside the main connurbations who have not been acquired by the larger retail chains.

But never before had I realised the extent of that tail and its consequences. The 983 customers who produce under 50 thousand cases are 37% of our total of 2,658 yet are producing only 6.1% of volume. Steve also pointed out that the bottom two categories – all those 1,612 customers to whom we sell under 100 thousand cases per annum – are 61% of the total profile yet produce only 7,561 thousand cases or 12.6% of total volume.

Henry's defensiveness was, I suppose, predictable even though Steve and Bob had gone out of their way to stress that the figures were not meant to be a direct criticism of him and his department. But his attitude was so aggressive that Bob Palmer had to intervene to support Steve and the whole atmosphere became combative. And, from that point, there was no way Henry could win – these people were far too sharp for him and he should have accepted it.

"We spend very little time on servicing the small customers," said Henry.

Steve then produced an analysis which showed that 37% of sales representatives' call time was spent servicing the 61% of customers who produced only 12.6% of volume.

"Well, we only call on the way home from bigger customers," said Henry but nobody really believed him.

"Small customers will become the large ones of tomorrow," said Henry.

Steve produced an analysis which showed that, of the small customers of three years ago, not one had risen significantly – they were all small businesses who would stay that way.

"We always charge higher prices for small orders," said Henry.

Steve produced an analysis which showed that, though the contribution margins on small customers were marginally higher than average, it was not that significant. Indeed he went on to show that, when you worked out the average cost per call of a salesperson based on typical monthly cost and activity, the contribution from customers producing less than 50,000 cases did not even cover the cost of the sales time spent calling on them.

Henry was particularly defensive about the salespeople's call cost and made all sorts of nit-picking queries, totally missing the point that this was strategic cost analysis and was only giving broad indications of cost levels so that long-term options for action could be considered. I just let Henry get on with it now, convinced in my mind that he had to go, rather cynically realising that this continued behaviour would only persuade others of the justification of my decision.

The problem has been that the legacy of Henry's attitude and the vacuum since he left, have made it difficult to move towards any plan of action in the same way as we have with the product range. Bob and Steve's full profitability analysis, worked out on a similar basis to the product profile, showed that we lose money on customers below 100,000 cases a year and the breakeven point is around 150,000.

In the circumstances I've decided to leave things until Henry's successor is appointed. Clearly there are a number of options. We can price small orders, and therefore small customers, at higher levels though this will not solve the problem on its own. We can refuse to take on small customers but this presents real problems in practice and is best achieved through a minimum order size. We can also use distributors for orders and customers under a certain level though we would be bound to lose some of our margin.

But all this will have to be linked to a complete re-organisation of the sales force and a cost reduction plan which will extend way beyond the sales function. Removing small customers will enable substantial savings in distribution and administration but a lot of work needs to be done on the detail. Steve also pointed out that there was an interesting correlation between small products and small customers which would justify linking the two cost reduction programmes together.

Chris is taking on responsibility for carrying on the work started by the internal audit team and she is doing some preparatory evaluations of cost reduction potential. But full implementation needs to wait for the new VP Sales and I've been very disappointed with the calibre of those put forward by the Executive Headhunters we engaged. I mention my concern to Al.

"The problem seems to be this," I say, "most of the men we've seen are like Henry. They've come through the ranks as good salesmen and then they've been promoted. They've had very little training and the main skills they've developed are social and interpersonal ones. Yet we want someone who has these skills but is also numerate and analytical with a business-like approach. Someone who can hold his own with the buyers of the top retailers and also appreciate the importance of the sort of analysis which Steve and Bob did for us. I just wonder if such people exist, looking at this lot." I flick through the application forms. "What do you think Al?"

"Well Phil," replies Al, "If you want me to be honest, I

do think you're being over optimistic. You want a person who's had some kind of MBA training yet who's also had a lot of experience on the sales side. They may exist but they're few and far between. Most of the best MBAs go into marketing or finance like Chris did or get a job in Wall Street. Most of the people in other functions are like Henry, Jane and John – they've made it without any formal business training. The only exceptions are those who've done what I'm aiming for – to get a part-time MBA while still doing their job. And it's tough I can tell you."

A sudden thought comes to my mind, one that maybe could solve our problem in a most unexpected way. But I decide to leave it for the time being.

"But the person I need doesn't have to be an MBA Al. I just want him or her to have a broad business awareness, something which is more to do with attitude than academic ability. But this lot we've interviewed so far – they seem so narrow and so unbusinesslike."

"Phil, could it be because over here there's a much bigger separation between those who've had business training and those who haven't? From what you've told me about the UK, you seem to have quite a lot of short, in-company courses but there aren't too many around in the US. If you don't take the initiative and get yourself an MBA, you can get left behind. I saw myself as being cut off in the Personnel function with no prospects of going anywhere else in the business. So I decided to do something about it."

Some time during this year I must get some business awareness training organised in the company so that the younger managers in sales and other functions don't become like Henry. I think that Chris would enjoy organising that – she has such a talent for helping others to understand business issues. I mention this to Al and he's highly enthusiastic.

But now I have the shorter-term problem of finding Henry's successor and I think that maybe Al's mind is working the same way as mine. He certainly seems to be throwing out one or two hints so I decide to confront him. He's sitting by my side, looking down at the pile of application forms – young, able, enthusiastic, business-like – someone I can work with very well.

"Al," I say, "maybe we're approaching this recruitment the wrong way. We've assumed that we need someone with a sales background who also has analytical and business skills. We could be making the same classic mistake as we made with Henry – choosing a good salesman and making him an inadequate sales manager. Do you see what I'm getting at Al?"

"I think so Phil but I'd like you to be more specific."

"OK Al, I'll put my cards on the table. Not one of the people we've seen so far would do the job as well as you. You've got the people management skills and you're very much respected by the sales side here, particularly since Henry left. You've shown your flair for business most impressively since you started your MBA course and I know you're numerate and analytical. The only thing you lack is a track record in sales and we've been assuming that this is essential. But I'm not so sure. We think much too much in functional boxes. I believe that, with the support and expertise of Jim Hooker to carry out the routine management of the sales force and also with my backing, you could be the VP Sales that Chapmans need."

He smiles at me and I can see from the expression in his eyes that this is the challenge he needs. I've always believed that, of all the skills needed to be successful in business, enthusiasm is probably the most vital and Al will certainly provide this. He looks so pleased with himself that I wonder if my idea was quite such a surprise to him.

"Phil," he says, "you sure do make up your mind quickly. But yes I'd love the challenge. Thanks for asking me."

We shake hands. I pick up the application forms and throw them into my out-tray with an exaggerated flourish. I know I've taken an impulsive decision but something deep inside tells me that I'm doing the right thing. This is a move that will help to change the culture of the sales function and get everyone at Chapmans to begin to think outside conventional career boxes.

Al and I then begin to discuss the implications of this

move for his own function.

He has a very good Assistant, Catherine, who is titled Personnel Officer and we decide that she can take on most of Al's present responsibilities with the title of Personnel Manager. I suggest that Al continues to take a close interest in the cost reduction programme associated with product rationalisation because we are anticipating a few redundancies on the production side within the next few months. As Al describes his main priorities at the moment, I can see that his present job is providing him with few new challenges anyway. He's obviously got things well organised on the personnel side and they will tick over fairly easily when he moves out.

Just then Karen comes in to tell me that Christine and Jane are waiting outside and I remember that the three of us agreed to meet to discuss pricing, something which the Internal Auditors said we should look at in certain product areas. Al and I agree to meet the following day to discuss the timing and announcement of his appointment.

Chris and Jane come in as he leaves, the two of them representing a real contrast in every way: Christine, fairly tall, blonde, slim, full of confidence; Jane small, dark, well rounded and, despite her natural assertiveness, finding it hard to establish herself in her new role of VP Marketing. Like Henry, she took some stick from the Internal Auditors and initially she disappointed me with her defensive attitude. But, unlike Henry, she's been willing to learn and to change.

Chris looks happy and relaxed as she comes towards me and our eyes meet in that special way that's only possible when people care for each other as much as we do. And, right now, our relationship is on a high, a far too passionate high if I'm honest with myself. We had a rough time in December – we had some cross words after the Internal Auditors meeting when I felt that she was supporting them against me. And then there was the Christmas and New Year holiday period which poses particular problems for those having illicit affairs. We both wanted to be together but I also wanted to be with my family and, anyway, could not find a realistic excuse for being away from them.

In many ways it was a great holiday for the family. The children continue to love everything about the life over here and it was the relaxed, loving Christmas which I used to dream about when Jean and I were separated. But the yearning to be with Chris was there all the time and made me feel that I was going through the motions with Jean. And, though nothing has yet been said, I feel that she's going through the motions too. She seems to have a distant, far-away look in her eyes which convinces me that she knows what I'm up to. Yet still I love her, or certainly feel very fond of her, and our relationship, in and out of bed, continues much as before. The pleasing thing is that, for the time being, the children seem to have no idea that there is any problem.

But last weekend was a turning point and has convinced me that, before too long, Chris and I are going to have to make up our minds about the future. I went to attend a Food Manufacturers' Association Conference in Washington and, unknown to anyone else, Chris came down to the Hotel and spent Friday and Saturday night with me. Somehow being away from Chapmans and our normal home environment relaxed us both and our sexual relationship reached new heights. We also talked a lot, through most of Friday night, and agreed that, at some point, we will need to go public about our affair – we are deceiving too many people at present and it can't go on for ever.

In the end we agreed to give it six months and then see if we both feel the same. If so, we'll tell Jean, the children and everyone at Chapmans. I wanted a shorter time but Chris insisted that we both really have to be sure if we are to make such a traumatic decision.

I know she's right but the indescribable joy of holding such a beautiful woman in my arms for those two nights makes it very hard to wait that long. It also makes it very hard to be rational – otherwise how could I be considering breaking up such a loving family for the second time? But I'm not sure I'm any longer in control and it's frightening.

As always with me, it seems that, as personal problems increase, my business career seems to thrive. The visit of the Internal Auditors – they're not really auditors, just very effective management consultants – has stimulated lots of ideas to improve things and Chris has used their visit as a catalyst to start off many of the ideas she picked up at McKenzies. I've been impressed with the fact that she's not worried about the Auditors taking the credit, she's just gone ahead and done things.

One particularly useful system she's introduced is the evaluation of capital projects to see if the cash flows which were projected have been achieved – POST AUDIT as it is termed in ABT. Bob and Steve recommended that Chris should produce a number of evaluations for ABT, justifying major capital expenditures over the last three years.

I did mention to Chris and to Bob Palmer at the final meeting where we agreed the content of their report to ABT, that we've only had proper evaluation methods at Chapmans since I introduced Discounted Cash Flow techniques soon after I came over with Richard. Prior to that, decisions seem to have been taken on a 'gut feel' basis. If somebody wanted a machine, they usually got it without having to justify the investment by projecting cash flows and expected return.

But Chris and Bob – who continued to work very closely together throughout the Auditors stay – convinced me that producing a DCF evaluation was only part of the process. You must then follow it up with a post project comparison. At first I argued that this was difficult and not always helpful because it was usually impossible to reverse a major investment several years later.

"Of course you're right Phil," said Bob with Chris, to my irritation, nodding while looking at him admiringly, "but just because something is difficult it doesn't mean you don't try. And, even if the investment is now impossible to unravel, that's not the point. What it does is create a climate where people think more carefully about their assumptions."

"It's already happening Phil," said Chris. "Ever since Bob and Steve raised the issue, I've noticed that John Madden is taking a totally different view about his capital proposals and is asking which past projects are likely to be investigated."

After that meeting I agreed that Chris could take one project on a pilot basis and see what we get from a post audit evaluation. We chose the installation of a new production line three years ago. It was one of the first projects we evaluated on a DCF basis and the whole case was based on extra sales volume of what was then a new product for us – Breakfast Waffles.

As Chris now walks into my office with Jane for the pricing meeting, she says, "Here's the post audit evaluation on the Waffles line Phil. I think you'll find it interesting to say the least. Can we discuss it some time tomorrow?"

I agree to read it overnight and see Chris after tomorrow's morning meeting. But now we concentrate on pricing. Chris and Jane have already had a previous meeting to isolate certain products where it may be possible to move up prices without disastrous marketing implications. But I remain fairly sceptical. I've always believed that pricing is a marketing issue much more than a financial one because it is part of the marketing mix which conveys the overall message about the product. I've always been very reluctant to sacrifice market share for any short-term financial gain, based not just on experience but also on some of the marketing theory I've picked up over the years. One theme is constantly heard from research old and new – there is a strong correlation between market share and long-term profitability. I make these points to Chris and Jane as the meeting starts and I can see that Jane is pleased – she obviously has similar reservations.

"No-one is going to question your ultimate responsibility for pricing Phil – I accept that it has to be a marketing issue. But all Bob was saying" – why does she keep bringing his name into it? I say to myself – "is that we should at least look at the options. Because ultimately it's the trade-off between price and volume which is important and we should therefore have a good knowledge of the price elasticity of the products we sell into our various markets."

I'm just going to get Chris to explain 'elasticity' when I suddenly understand what she means. As so often happens, the word – which I recall from when I studied economics at nightschool to please Old Man Lawrence in my early days at Lawrensons – obscures the simplicity of the concept. Elasticity of demand is the extent to which volume will be affected by a price change. If price goes up by 10% and volume falls by 10%, that is elasticity of one or 'Unity' as they used to call it. If volume goes down very substantially following a price increase (or goes up following a price reduction), that is a very elastic price/volume relationship. If there is little impact on volume, that is inelastic and these are the obvious candidates for price increases.

Chris goes on to say that she and Jane have chosen certain products as potentially inelastic and that Jane has made an estimate of the likely impact on volume of price increases of between 2 and 10%.

"I should say that these are very much estimates Phil," says Jane, "and you may also want to give your view on the likely impact. I'm not sure that you'll even be willing to consider a price increase in some cases, particularly Waffles, where we're still trying to build up our market share and it's highly competitive."

I wonder if Chris has told Jane about the Waffles post audit appraisal, but of course she wouldn't have shown her the results without letting me see them first. I now see some interesting relationships between these more advanced approaches to management accounting. I recall that several Waffle products were in the bottom section of the product range profile which was showing a loss. I also suspect that Chris's post audit evaluation will show that the required DCF return has not been achieved. Thus Waffles need to deliver higher profitability and one way is to look at price. I begin to understand that, though I thought I knew all about management accounting after my time with Chris at Lawrensons, I had only scratched the surface. I saw a range of techniques like costing, investment appraisal and budgetary control. Now I'm seeing an integrated approach to analysing business problems.

Chris now writes up some figures on the flipchart:

WAFFLES – SIX PACK	$000
Sales price per 000 cases	8,620
Variable costs	5,130
Contribution	3,490

"OK Jane. Now this represents the standard costings we've been using on this product this year and I don't think raw material price changes have had a major impact. The other variable costs are labour, energy, distribution and promotional expenses."

"What about repairs and maintenance Chris?" I ask, "I thought we always included these as variable too."

"We used to Phil but I got one of our management accountants to do an analysis soon after I arrived and it tends to be more fixed than variable. John generally works to planned maintenance schedules which are fixed in the short term."

"Did you examine any of the other costs Chris?" comes in Jane, "because I have some doubts about labour. A lot of our people are on basic fixed salaries which don't change with volume."

"Yes Jane, we had a look at them all and the situation varies a lot between factories. It also varies depending on the extent of the volume change. So it's never a black and white split. But I'm satisfied that, on balance, labour, energy, distribution and promotion costs tend to vary with volume in a fairly direct way, within a budget period. Though the way it happens may be in a series of little steps."

She turns to the flipchart and draws a graph which I recall her drawing at Lawrensons, during one of our first sessions together.

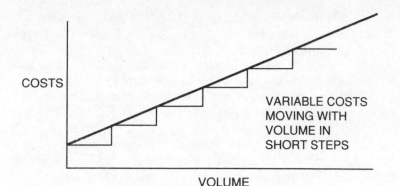

I mention my recollection to Chris.

"Yes Phil, but then I was using the step graph to illustrate the point that most fixed costs move in steps with volume over a period of years. So you could say that this graph shows how variable costs move in steps with small volume changes over a period of months, whereas fixed costs move with large volume changes over a period of years."

"Do all fixed costs move with volume over a period of years then?" I ask, feeling that this discussion is bringing out some new insights which haven't really occurred to me before.

"Most do Phil but not all. In fact the distinction between those two types of fixed costs is something I want to take up with you some other time. I did some interesting work at McKenzies on strategic cost analysis which I think could be useful when we review our competitive position."

"I didn't know we were going to do that Chris," I say, looking at Jane with a conspiratorial wink, "but I'm sure you'll put it on my agenda when you're ready."

It is typical of our present good relationship that my irony is taken as it was intended – as a bit of fun.

"Sure Phil," she says, "I'd like both of you to be involved of course – with Henry's successor too I hope."

I take them both into my confidence about Al's appointment and they are both surprised but delighted. Chris says how ideal he will be and can't understand why she didn't think of it. Jane says that it will be so much easier working with someone who knows the business and the people so well.

Chris, with typical task orientation, brings us back to the purpose of the meeting and the figures on her flipchart.

"Now I asked Jane for her best prediction of what would happen to volume if we put up price by 10%, assuming no increases in unit variable costs," says Chris, "but, first of all, let's have a look at the impact on contribution if we put our prices up by 10%, with no loss of volume. I know that's probably unrealistic but this is just the first stage."

She writes up:

WAFFLES		Price + 10%
Sales price per 000 cases	8,620	9,482
Variable Costs	5,130	5,130
Contribution	3,490	4,352

"So you can see that the 10% price increase goes straight to the contribution line and increases it by $862 for a thousand cases," explains Chris in her usual lucid way.

Jane then asks a question which makes me realise how much she still has to learn about financial matters and convinces me even more of the need for some management training courses.

"But why have you left out the fixed costs Chris, don't we want to see the impact on net profit rather than just contribution?"

"We've left them out because they aren't going to change as a result of this decision Jane. Thus any change in contribution will go straight through to the bottom line of profit. The whole point of separating variable costs and calculating contributions is that they represent the change factors we need to analyse. If prices go up and volume falls, total fixed costs will not change."

Jane nods in apparent agreement but I wonder if she really appreciates what Chris is saying. I can never understand why this simple, basic point is so difficult for managers to appreciate. For short-term, tactical decisions, you focus on the things which change in the short term. It's only when you're into more strategic evaluations – like the product and customer profile analysis – that you bring in fixed costs.

"Now Phil, Jane believes you would lose 10% of volume if she put up prices by 10%. What do you think?"

"Hmm, Unity," I say, hoping Chris will be impressed by my recollection of the term from my days of O level economics. "Yes I'd go along with that. We'd lose a few orders but we'd just about hold our turnover levels I should think."

"But I'd still be very concerned about losing 10% market share Chris," intervenes Jane. "We're still trying very hard to establish our brand in Waffles and it's very competitive. So I don't see the point if we're only holding turnover at the same level."

"Do you see the point Phil?" asks Chris.

She's putting me on the spot but such is my confidence in my management accounting knowledge these days that I don't really mind. I know that it's not as simple as Jane is saying. We'll be better off in contribution terms because of the way variable costs will behave but I'm not able to work it out in my head. Instead I say, "I can see what you're getting at Chris. The sales side, who are targeted on turnover, will say 'Why bother?' and Jane is obviously thinking that way too. But I would like to see your re-calculation of contribution because I've a feeling we're going to be surprised."

"I think you are Phil," says Chris and writes up figures which make Jane catch her breath and confirm my expectation that I had underestimated the likely impact on profit.

Chris now adds to the figures:

WAFFLES		Price + 10%	Volume – 10% (900 cases)
Sales price per 000 cases	8,620	9,482	8,534
Variable Costs	5,130	5,130	4,617
Contribution	3,490	4,352	3,917

"Now let me stress to both of you," says Chris, "that I'm still not necessarily suggesting that you go ahead and put the price up because that's a marketing issue. But I would like you to consider the potential short-term impact on profit if you are right about losing only 10% volume."

"Could you please explain the 8,534 and the 4,617 Chris?" asks Jane, "I'm not sure how you've arrived at them."

"I've reduced them both by 10% Jane – the 9,482 and the 5,130 less 10% gives you 8,534 and 4,617 respectively. You would sell 10% less cases so your turnover is more or less where you started, less than 100 down, but the variable costs are reduced by 10% because you're producing less volume and therefore require less material, labour, energy and other costs which reduce in line with volume. OK?"

"Oh," says Jane, still uncertain and I decide to intervene while she's pondering the figures.

"Which makes your division between fixed and variable costs more than an academic exercise Chris. We have to be sure that if volume of Waffles did fall by 10%, you really would be able to reduce all those variable costs, directly and immediately. And I'd need to be convinced about labour, not just generally but for Waffles in particular."

"I hear..." I know that Chris was going to say 'I hear what you say' but she stops herself because she knows how much I detest the phrase. I pull a friendly face at her and we silently enjoy the in-joke while Jane looks puzzled. "I know what you mean Phil and I will check out the position on all these variable costs if we do go ahead. But I'm satisfied that they are more variable than fixed and it can never be a black and white division."

Jane is sitting studying the figures with interest.

"I'd no idea about this before Chris and I'm amazed. Is it the same for all products?" Again I'm surprised at the naïveté of Jane's question and I'm thinking of replying myself but I decide to leave it to Chris – she does explain these things so much better than me.

"Not exactly the same Jane. It all depends on the proportion of variable costs to sales. The figure before the price increase 5,130 on 8,620 is nearly 60% which is quite high compared with the average. That's why it has such a favourable impact on contribution – you're saving such a lot of variable cost when volume falls. There will always be a positive impact on contribution from a plus 10% minus 10% situation but the extent depends on the variable cost to sales ratio."

Having satisfied myself that Jane has grasped all this, because I know how important this understanding is to her job, I then move on to another point that has just occurred to me. One thing I enjoy about these sessions with Chris is that I feel I'm both learning and contributing. I also feel that Chris, despite her obvious flair and grasp of the subject, is learning too – maybe it's because this whole area of management accounting is still developing and we're all on a learning curve together.

"Chris," I ask, "wouldn't it be interesting to work out a sort of breakeven point – the amount which volume could fall after a 10% price increase and still get back to our original contribution?"

"Yes Phil, that should be easy enough." She gets her calculator out while saying, "I really ought to have these on a spreadsheet. I could easily fix it on your PC Jane."

She then writes up:

WAFFLES	Price + 10%	Volume – 10% (900 cases)	Volume – 20% (800 cases)
Sales price per 000 cases 8,620	9,482	8,534	7,586
Variable Costs	5,130 5,130	4,617	4,104
Contribution	3,490 4,352	3,917	3,482

"So it's near enough 20% Phil. If price went up by 10% with no loss of volume it would give you contribution of 4,352 but this would be reduced by 20% to 3,482 if both sales and variable costs went down by 20%. Remember Jane," I notice that she addresses this point only to her and not to me which fills me with some kind of confidence, "that contribution is sales less variable costs so if both of them go down by 20%, so will the contribution."

"In some ways I prefer to think of it that way Chris," says Jane. "What could we afford to lose after a price increase and still be no worse off? If my PC could calculate that for every product, it would be very helpful."

Jane then continues with a comment which makes me sure that she too is developing her confidence and joining in the learning curve.

"What about price reductions Chris? I would be interested to see similar calculations and to see if the reverse applies. If we bring down the price of Waffles by 10% – and I'm only using this as an example – and then gain 10% volume, what would be the impact? And how much would I need to get back to the same contribution?"

Chris offers her pen to Jane and asks her to make the calculation. I recall that Chris has always preferred to get others involved in this kind of evaluation rather than just doing it herself while we all watch.

"Just write up the cost structure of Waffles and then do what I did first – calculate the impact of the price reduction without any change in volume," says Chris.

Jane writes up:

WAFFLES		Price – 10%
Sales price per 000 cases	8,620	7,758
Variable Costs	5,130	5,130
Contribution	3,490	2,628

Jane and I look at these figures with surprise – surprise which wouldn't have been felt if we'd thought about it more carefully. Price reductions go straight down to the bottom line and the impact of a 10% reduction – 862 – is that much more significant when applied to the already low contribution made by Waffles. I see how futile it is to use price reductions to improve the position of low margin products, even if the volume increase is substantial. I had already accepted this in principle, but now I see it in the stark terms of bottom line impact.

I don't think Jane is yet seeing this in quite such clear terms because she's still laboriously working through the impact of the 'Unity' assumption in reverse – the effect of a 10% volume increase after the assumed 10% price reduction. She's amazed how poor the impact on contribution proves to be:

WAFFLES		Price – 10%	Volume + 10% (1100 cases)
Sales price per 000 cases	8,620	7,758	8,534
Variable Costs	5,130	5,130	5,643
Contribution	3,490	2,628	2,891

I get out my own calculator to check what is necessary to get back to the 3,490 contribution and, at first, I think I've made a mistake. To get from 2,628 back to 3,490 requires just under 33% increase in volume to compensate for a 10% reduction in price. I think of all our promotions which involve price reductions and wonder how many times I've authorised offers and discounts which did not produce the volume to cover their cost. While I'm thinking about this and how it emphasises the importance of having good financial advice available, Chris is explaining the 33% volume increase to Jane.

"So, to get back to the original contribution you were making before the price increase – 3,490 – you've got to increase it from 2,628 which is obviously a much higher increase than 10%. And if you calculate 3,490 as a percentage of 2,628, it's about 133%, hence you need a 33% volume increase to compensate for a 10% price reduction."

"But why Chris?" says Jane, obviously still having problems with the significance of variable costs and their impact on profitability.

"Because the 10% price reduction goes straight down to the bottom line and the volume increase only has an impact at the margin after variable costs. You have to spend all that money on variable costs if volume increases and therefore the impact of various price/volume combinations depends on the proportion of variable costs to sales. Remember that Waffles have fairly high variable costs so you need a much higher increase to compensate for a loss of volume than for other products."

Chris and Jane then go on to discuss the details of how a spreadsheet on her PC could be programmed to tell her the volume required to compensate for different percentage price reductions on each product and I think about ways in which we might institute a promotion evaluation procedure before we authorise any future special price reduction offers. I decide to discuss this with Chris later.

Just then Karen comes in and says, "Phil, Jean's on the phone and it sounds urgent."

"Put her through then."

Karen then comes up to me and whispers. "I think you'd better take it in my office Phil, she sounds very upset."

I feel that awful sensation in the pit of your stomach when suddenly you know that something is very wrong. As I walk towards the outer office, I see Chris look up at me with an expression of concern. She follows me to the door.

I pick up the phone and can tell instantly from Jean's voice that she is more than upset, she's devastated.

"Darling," her voice trembles, "it's Mark. He's had an accident at school. He dived into the swimming pool and has done something awful to his head and neck."

"How bad is it love?"

"He's in intensive care and they say it's touch and go."

"I'll be over straight away love. I know it's silly to say it but try not to worry. I'll be with you soon."

As I put the phone down, I find that my hand won't stop shaking. I tell Chris and Karen what has happened and look for my car keys. Karen says she's got them and, while she goes to her desk, Chris says, "Phil, please let me drive you there."

"No it's all right Chris, I'll be fine, honestly."

"Where is he – which hospital?"

I suddenly remember that I have not asked Jean and this convinces Chris that she needs to take charge. She takes my car keys and asks Karen to ring the school to find out where Mark is, then to call down to my carphone. There's no point in arguing and I feel happy that Chris is going to be with me.

But just as we drive out of the parking lot and Karen confirms the hospital location, it suddenly dawns on me what is going to happen. My wife will meet my mistress for the first time since my affair with Chris started. And though Mark's accident is the main thing on my mind, I also have a feeling that things are really going to come to a head now.

Chapter 16

It's a week later and I'm back in my office for my first normal working day since Mark's accident. He's just been taken off the danger list and at last we can begin to lead a normal life again. We also heard last night that there will be no long-term damage to his brain though I guess both Jean and I are going to be worried about this for some time to come. He was, after all, out cold for twelve hours and you're bound to wonder after that.

But he seemed fine when we saw him last night, apart from a massive headache and the fact that he can't remember anything at all of the day when his accident took place. Apparently, he dived into the shallow end of the school pool as he has done many times before but somehow got the angle wrong. Fortunately, two close friends were nearby and managed to get him out and call for help quickly.

Both Jean and I have been in a terrible state of anxiety and have very much turned back towards each other this last week. We've both appreciated the closeness and the mutual dependence which has always been part of our relationship when the chips are down. My concern about Chris seeing Jean at the hospital seems pathetically shallow now – Chris came with me and they exchanged smiles but Jean was hardly in a state to notice, never mind care.

Now though, a week later, I can think more objectively about how much more difficult this kind of family trauma is when you're having an affair, particularly when you're thinking of leaving your family. I question whether I could ever bring myself to do it when I have a wife who's so loyal and children who value so much the security of their home and their parents' relationship. Somehow during the last week my affair with Chris seems peripheral to the really important things in my life.

I haven't discussed this with Chris, nor do I want to at present. We've hardly spoken except for the odd message concerning work and she is behaving as the concerned and dependable friend of the family which she used to be. I find myself wishing more and more that this is what she could be again.

Chris is due to see me this morning to catch up on outstanding issues, including the post audit on the Waffles investment which we never got round to discussing because of Mark's accident. She starts off by asking me how Mark is and I can tell that this crisis puts her in a difficult position too. Our agreement not to talk about my family can't be continued and discussing Mark's condition and the impact on Jean, Angie and me, reminds us both of what we have been planning to do. We're quite pleased to change the subject and bury ourselves in the Waffles post audit.

Chris has brought along the original Capital Proposal which I approved three years ago. I remember the figures quite well as it was one of my first projects at Chapmans and one to which I had a great deal of emotional attachment. I mention this to Chris and she gives me a rather critical look before saying, "That's interesting Phil, because the sales volume forecast, which was by far the most sensitive assumption in the project, was very optimistic. It can be a real problem if you're emotionally involved and trying to get your project through – sometimes you cease to be realistic."

"Unless there's someone like you to bring me back to reality?"

"Yes Phil. I don't think anyone else in the accounting function here would have done that. They would have said, and I think would still say, that sales forecasts are your affair not theirs. They all tend to see their roles as just to add up the numbers. I'm trying to change the attitudes but it's a long haul."

"And what would you have done Chris, or what will you do on future occasions? Because though I couldn't value you more highly as my CFO, you still don't know as much about the potential of new products as me or Jane. Not that we always know as much as we ought to."

"Well there are two main things Phil and I'm already doing this with Jane. Firstly I can question all the assumptions closely and maybe help you to understand where you need more information. Chapmans always seem to have been reluctant to invest in market research and I think it's false economy. Secondly I can work out some sensitivities on the computer – what if you're wrong by 5 or maybe 10% on your volume assumption? How would it affect the return? I think you would have thought much more carefully about Waffles if you'd have known how vulnerable it was to even a small loss of volume."

"All this is obviously building up to the fact that the post audit shows I made a cock-up," I say resignedly. "You'd better show me the worst."

"OK Phil, let's have a look at the original capital proposal."

Cash Flow before discounting ($000)

Year	Plant & Equipment	R & D	Sales	Variable Costs	Distribution	Incremental Marketing	Fixed Costs Advertising	Net Cash Flow
0	−120	−16						−136
1			+500	−250	−50	−60	−150	−10
2			+700	−330	−60	−100	−190	+20
3			+800	−360	−70	−100	−200	+70
4			+900	−380	−80	−130	−230	+80
5			+1000	−400	−90	−130	−270	+110
	−120	−16	+3900	−1720	−350	−520	−1040	+134

I look down at the cash flow which, when discounted, gave us a DCF Return of 22%, well above what we were looking for at the time.

I recall, with some guilt and regret, how arbitrary were some of the assumptions behind these figures. I turn to the second page marked 'assumptions' and read the words which seemed so credible when I put them forward to Richard in my early days at Chapmans.

- Sales price to start at average $8 per case, rising to $9 dollars in year 2, stabilising at $9 thereafter.

- Volume to be 62,500 cases in year 1, 78,000 in year 2, rising by 11,000 cases per annum for each year thereafter.

- Variable costs to be 50% of sales, reducing progressively to 40% over the five year period.

- Product Manager in year 1, Marketing assistants recruited in years 2 and 4.

- Advertising to be confined to in-store promotion, no TV exposure.

I look for any reference to assumptions on distribution costs but can't find any. I notice that the distribution figures look even more approximate than the others and I seem vaguely to recall that we added $10,000 a year to the cash flow because no-one could provide any accurate data on the likely cost behaviour following the expected volume increases. I feel it would be better to keep quiet about that and hope that Chris doesn't question it. I'm quite sure that she'll have quite enough to question in her post audit comparison, without bothering with this relatively small and difficult cost.

I am certainly right about this. Chris produces a comparison which shows an even worse position than I'd feared.

It reads like this:

Sales Comparison

	Volume (cases)		Price per case		Sales (approx)	
	Project	Actual	Project	Actual	Project	Actual
Year 1	62,500	51,000	$8.00	$8.00	500,000	408,000
Year 2	78,000	64,000	$9.00	$8.30	700,000	531,000
Year 3	89,000	68,000	$9.00	$8.62	800,000	586,000

I look at this comparison and understand how important it is for me to be made to confront the awful reality of this project, however uncomfortable it may feel. I knew it was bad but not this bad! Then Chris makes an important point which enables me to see things in a different, even more uncomfortable light.

"There are many problems with this kind of evaluation Phil because it's so difficult to isolate one project in a complex business. You'll see that particularly when we come to look at the cost position. But, though sales are fairly easy to isolate, there is the problem of inflation."

"But we left inflation out of the cash flows Chris. I remembered from Lawrensons how you told me to leave it out because it made the numbers very big in later years and made the DCF return appear higher than it otherwise would be."

"Yes Phil, that's right and I'm pleased you've remembered it. But I've had much wider experience since then and I've come to see the value of post audit. I now believe it is probably best to do cash flows both ways, with and without inflation."

"But why Chris? Isn't it just making things too complicated?"

"Maybe it's complicated Phil and maybe it's something we don't need to publish too widely within Chapmans. But just think about that price comparison above. You are now charging $8.62 dollars 3 years after the project assumptions. Inflation over here has been about 10% in total over the three year period. So the comparison really ought to be with the $9 you assumed in the evaluation plus 10% – nearly $10. Thus you've lost even more on price than it appears. Hence the importance of our price/volume calculations last week."

Again I see the links between the various management accounting approaches Chris is using. The post audit stimulates us to review price; the price/volume evaluation helps us to assess the implications. If price changes are not likely to be feasible, then we have to look at the possibility of getting out of the Waffles market altogether, which will require a specific evaluation of the avoidable costs and the overall impact on profit and cash flow. And all these management accounting approaches need to be complemented by the marketing and strategic judgement which only Jane and I can provide.

I am just about to raise this with Chris but she's already moved on to the cost schedule. I'm beginning to be worried about time, remembering that I promised to be home for lunch so we can visit Mark this afternoon and also remembering that I've got about a week's mail to go through with Karen.

"Can you just take me through the main points Chris and tell me the ... bottom line." Our eyes meet as I use this phrase – one we always used to laugh about at Lawrensons because it became a symbol of my previous ignorance of financial matters. The look in her eyes reminds me that she isn't just a family friend and that there's no way we can ever go back to that situation.

"OK Phil. Well, in this case, I've adjusted the original project cost to include inflation. So they are expressed in today's values which means that the comparison with today's costs is valid."

"So you've added on the 10% inflation that's taken place since we authorised the project?"

"More or less – if I know a different figure, like management salaries which is nearer 15%, I've taken that instead."

			Incremental Fixed Costs				
	Variable Costs	Distribution	Marketing	Advertising	Total Fixed Costs	Total Costs
	Project Actual	Project Actual	Project Actual	Project Actual	Project Actual	Project Actual
Year 1	250 212	50 50	60 52	150 162	260 264	510 476
Year 2	347 260	63 63	107 103	200 231	370 397	717 657
Year 3	396 270	77 77	115 114	220 202	412 393	808 663

I look back to the sales figures on the previous page and I see the true awfulness of the situation. Chris sees what I'm doing and intervenes.

"Phil. Just take a look at the next page. It gives the summary project position."

I turn over the page and see:

SUMMARY OF ACTUAL RESULTS

	Year 1	Year 2	Year 3	TOTAL
Sales	408,000	531,000	586,000	1,525,000
Costs	476,000	657,000	663,000	1,796,000
Cash flow	− 68,000	− 126,000	− 77,000	− 271,000

Note

In addition to the above, the initial estimate of expenditure on plant of £120,000 was overspent by £21,000 and research costs before launch were £20,000 rather than £16,000.

"So we even overspent on our initial investment and no-one knew about it until now," I say, trying to express the concern I feel. "I see the problem Chris, looking back with hindsight. All the effort went into the DCF evaluation and getting it through. Then we just sat back – we thought we'd done it. There was no control at all on what actually happened."

"Which is why we must institute post audit on a regular basis Phil."

"Yes Chris, but that's not all. It's not just investment projects which we need to look at in this way, it's the profitability of all ongoing product groups. What frightens me most about this is that we have a product group which is losing money and I didn't know. I knew that individual Waffle products were making low contributions but I never knew that they weren't even covering their incremental costs. If I had known that I might have looked at price earlier or considered getting out altogether."

"So what would you like me to do Phil?"

"Well you're the expert Chris and I'm not sure how easy it is to organise but I would like to have a full profitability evaluation of all our major product groups every 6 months or so. Including all fixed costs which we can attribute to them."

"I can see the need Phil and I will look into it for you. But there'll need to be a lot of estimates when you get down to fixed costs. Waffles are easier than most because their production unit and their marketing operation are fairly self contained. But even there I had to make quite a lot of estimates, particularly with distribution which is one of the most difficult to split out."

"I don't mind about that Chris because all I want is guidance. As you've mentioned, I'm not suddenly going to ditch Waffles without further analysis."

I pause and try to think about what I really need to help my decision making – always the best way to decide on new information required by managers.

"Actually Chris, what I'd like you to do now is re-calculate the total profitability of the Waffles range assuming that the plus 10% price minus 10% volume change applies throughout. Then a specific evaluation of the fixed costs we'd actually save if we did pull out. Because, for instance, I'm not sure we'd really save that much on distribution costs in practice."

"But we would save advertising Phil – all that TV spend you said we'd never need for Waffles," she adds sarcastically, "but we'd only save Marketing if Jane is prepared to get rid of her Product Manager and the Assistant. But sure, I'll have a look at the total picture for you."

On balance I feel quite pleased with my morning's work. Though it started with the rather demoralising audit on the Waffles project, I feel that I've learned a lot and now look back with amazement at the way I've allowed things to drift on without considering the overall profitability of the venture. Chris is absolutely right to stress the virtues of post audit (though even she had to be prompted by the visit of the Auditors to introduce this) but I feel that I was able to add something by stressing the need to carry out regular profitability analyses on all major product groups.

The Auditors made a valuable contribution by encouraging special 'one-off' analyses like Pareto and Post Audit but I want Chris to establish systems which ensure that we can never again be losing money on a part of the business without being fully aware of it.

When I think about this and the reasons why it has happened, I see the disadvantage of the variable costing approach which Chris has always favoured and which I have followed her in advocating. Looking at individual products on a variable cost and contribution basis is fine for tactical evaluations to optimise profit in the short term, but sometimes someone has to sit back and say – What does all this mean for our long-term strategy? I mention this point to Chris, trying not to let her think that I'm blaming her too directly.

"Yes Phil," she says, "I've been thinking the same thing. I've changed my views a lot since my early days at Lawrensons, mainly because of what I learned at McKenzies. Much of their work was on strategic profitability analysis which companies usually fail to do themselves. And you're right to point out that, so far, I've been slow in getting round to looking at the profitability of product groups, except where Steve suggested it."

"Steve?"

"The Auditor – you know the little, dynamic one."

"Oh yes," I say. At least she isn't still thinking about Bob Palmer, I think to myself, that awful poseur with his film star looks and patronising manner. Though I know I'm being unfair, I can't help it. It was a wonderful sight when he finally completed the Audit and left with his little pal, the dynamic Steve, five foot nothing in his socks. They really did look a funny pair yet I have to admit they've done a lot to change our thinking.

Chris is continuing to talk while I am miles away, enjoying my jealous, uncharitable thoughts about two men who were only doing the job they were sent to do.

"You see Phil," she says, "I think this area of strategic cost and profitability analysis is not one where you can come up with lots of easy labels and techniques like you can with basic management accounting. It's more a question of having an open and a curious mind, looking at the strengths and weaknesses of the business and trying to find the information which will help strategic decisions. And good analysis is likely to come from all of us being alive to new ideas. You've suggested regular product group profitability analysis – I've been doing some work recently on the Product Development Section of our Research function."

"Product development?" I say. "How can you evaluate that? Surely the people we have there are an investment in the future."

"Yes, but you can evaluate investments Phil. We do it all the time. I've just taken some fairly easily available data from our existing management information and the results are fascinating."

I look at my watch, 11.30 am already and I need to leave by 12 noon to get home for lunch.

"I'm a bit short of time Chris. Could you just give me the gist of it and leave the detail for me to study later."

"OK Phil. It won't take me a minute to write the essential facts on the flipchart and you can ponder them at your leisure. But we will need to address the issue with Jane and John Madden because I don't think they have any idea of the seriousness of the position."

As I look at Chris, this young, confident, perfectly gorgeous lady, I once again have to pinch myself to believe that we actually are having an affair and that she really does seem to prefer me to the Bob Palmers of this world, those of her own lifestyle and generation. Could it be that she's just using me for her career advancement? No – she could have got a dozen jobs like the one at Chapmans and, if she'd stayed at McKenzies, she would have earned far more money.

"Penny for your thoughts?" she says, noting my far away look.

"I was thinking about you Chris. About us, I guess. How amazing it is that you seem to care for me. Sorry love – I forgot – we shouldn't talk like this at work. Back to Product Development."

"I really do not understand you Phil. Or maybe I do. It seems that the more you succeed, the more insecure you become. The whole problem with you failing to understand financial matters at Lawrensons was lack of confidence and it seems to affect every part of your life. I don't know what I can do to make you relax? I do care for you but it gets much more difficult when you're like this. Now please can we finish this – I know you're in a hurry."

There's a touch of irritation in her voice and I realise how right she is. Insecurity, jealousy, paranoia – they're all there in my relationship with her. But it's easier to recognise than to resolve. My mind thankfully returns to other things as I see that Chris is producing yet another piece of devastating management information.

COMPARISON

* Amount spent on new product development
  per annum (average over last five years -
  today's prices) $7.2 m

* Contribution (before fixed costs) received
  this year from new products developed
  over last five years $5.9 m

"I don't believe it Chris. And this is before fixed costs too. You say that John and Jane haven't seen this yet?"

"No Phil. I thought I ought to show you first. I didn't need to consult them to get the information – it was all very easily available from regularly reported data but we'd never bothered to extract it before."

"It would be interesting to see some kind of breakdown, Chris. Like how it looks by different product groups for instance. I'm just beginning to see how little I know about this business yet I'm the one who's supposed to be running it."

"I just don't know what's available Phil, until I see John. I'm not sure how far he breaks down the time of his PD people but, whatever he does now, we must make sure we have full records for the future. This is something I want to monitor very closely for you."

"I can just imagine how John will react – you talk to Marketing he'll say. It's just another part of the jigsaw which the 80/20 and the post audit analyses have started to piece together – we just do not know which parts of the business are providing value for money."

"I think it links very closely to the 80/20 analysis Phil because this must mean that a lot of the PD work went into new products that just haven't achieved sufficient volume to justify the time spent developing them, never mind other costs. I must analyse how many of these new products are in the less than 100,000 cases per annum category. My guess is that there'll be a high proportion."

"Which means that ... ?" I say, suspecting the answer.

"Our cost reduction plans will probably need to encompass product development far more than we intended. I've tried so far to leave PD out as an essential investment but I think this could be a mistake."

"OK Chris, but let's be careful. I'd rather they focus their attention on more profitable activities. There's been too much marginal development of business with limited volume potential and not enough innovation into new product areas. That's what these figures are really saying. Let's fix up a meeting with John and Jane to discuss it further. You really do know how to stir things up don't you?"

"Maybe that's part of my job Phil and I hope I'll be able to continue to do it – in a positive way of course."

"Of course and I hope you will carry on doing so. I really need it – it's so easy to bury your head in day-to-day detail and lose sight of these longer-term issues."

I pick up my papers and pile them in the action tray on my desk. I hope this gives a clear message to Chris that I'm anxious to close the meeting. I must have a few minutes with Karen before I go home.

"Talking of longer-term issues Phil, there is something I'd like to suggest and I hope you won't be paranoid about it."

I think I know what's coming. I walk round from behind my desk and we're standing facing each other. I can see that she's nervous and swallowing hard.

"I guess it's happening anyway Phil. But I feel that, while you've got your family problems, we can't carry on as we have been. It just doesn't seem right. Can we agree to have a month or so without seeing each other outside work? It'll also give us time to think about the things we discussed in Washington, during our weekend together."

"What a weekend it was," is all I can find to say, a rather inadequate response.

"It was wonderful Phil. I can't remember a better one. But I find it difficult to deceive your family at any time but even more so now. Please can we just have a bit of space?"

I know she's right but it doesn't stop me feeling all kinds of regret. And the insecurity returns – has she got someone else? Is this just an excuse? But underneath there is also a strange feeling of relief.

"Of course Chris, darling."

I put my hands on her shoulders and kiss her on the lips. Suddenly the door opens and Karen walks in, says "Sorry" and walks out again.

"I just don't believe it," I say.

"I swear she's looking through the keyhole," says Chris. I think she's joking but she could be right.

I watch as Chris walks out of the room a few minutes later – those beautiful legs, the elegant walk, the long blonde hair seem to torment me as she moves towards the door.

I can't help feeling that the Christine I've known for the last few months is not going to come back.

Chapter 17

It is now exactly six months since that weekend Chris and I spent together in Washington. I know it's today because I've been counting the days in my mind ever since we decided to give it six months before taking the fateful step of going public about our affair. I sometimes think that cold, snowy weekend in Washington was the high point of our relationship which we've never managed to reach again. We've resumed our physical relationship now that Mark's over his accident and back at school but somehow it seems to have lost its spark.

I tell myself that it's because we're leading a secretive double life and that, when we've come out into the open, it will all be fine again. Incidents like Mark's accident are bound to make things difficult but once we've made our public commitment, we'll scale the peaks of Washington again.

I feel sure about this in my own mind but wish I could feel as confident about her. It is worrying that the expiry of the six month period has not been discussed between us. I've been reluctant to mention it and can't quite understand why; Chris seems to be deliberately avoiding it. I've decided that, sometime this week, I'll make sure we fix a time to talk it through.

This week is likely to be eventful for other reasons. Today we're having the much postponed meeting about the costing systems which our customers – the major retailers –

are using, something which Henry chose to ignore but which Al is keen to learn about. We're also having a meeting to review provisional half year results which, according to Chris's indications last week, look to be exceeding budget handsomely. Our new aggressive approach to pricing, Al's drive and energy on the sales side and the cost reduction programmes in parallel with the weeding out of small products and customers have all contributed to this improved performance. Matt Talbot's visits have become something I look forward to rather than dread because now I can proudly show the progress we are making towards the good financial performance that ABT require. I even got a congratulatory (if rather patronising) phone call from Arnold Kaufman last week and I have to admit that it felt good. Though I still believe I was rather misled by his promises at the time of the acquisition, life in ABT is nowhere near so bad as I first feared. In fact I'm rather enjoying it.

We're holding this meeting about costing systems in the retail business in the Board Room. As I enter, Chris is already there and is talking to Al about the improvements he wants to the customer profitability statements which we produce for all the major retailers. When I think about it, I suppose it's not too surprising that our customers are becoming more sophisticated about costing the products that they sell. After all, we do our own product costings so why shouldn't they? And we are trying to develop better information to help us in negotiations – hence the customer profitability statements – so we can't be too surprised if they try to retaliate.

Jane is sitting at the far end of the Board Room, going through some transparencies with Mike McDivett, the Brand Manager for our cookie range and someone who is making a name for himself very quickly at Chapmans. He's a pleasant lad but sometimes tries too hard to create an impression. He looks like something out of that Wall Street movie – plastered back hair, striped shirt, red braces and a staccato way of talking which would be more appropriate on the floor of a Wall Street dealing room. He's here because he joined us from Valumart and, while he was there, became closely involved with their product costing system. According to Chris, who came across these techniques at McKenzies, Valumart are further down the road than most other US retailers, the only one ahead of them being Pathway Supermarkets, the largest of all.

I was not aware that this meeting was going to start with a formal presentation but Mike and Jane have obviously planned it this way. Al, Chris and I settle down while Jane quickly sets the scene and then hands over to Mike. One thing which Jane says in her introduction really hits me between the eyes – apparently these developments have not just been led by retailers and consultants, they've been led by other manufacturers.

"The two most prominent have been Mars and Procter and Gamble," says Jane, "and they have used this for their own marketing benefit. They see competitive advantage in helping their customers to be more sophisticated in evaluating their profitability."

It becomes apparent to me just how narrowly I have been seeing this whole subject. I've seen it as a way of understanding how our customers make their decisions so we can second guess them in negotiations. The really progressive companies like Mars and P & G are seeing it as extra added value to offer their customers. How far we still have to go in our thinking. I hope Al is feeling the same way.

Mike McDivett stands up and continues to set the scene in a most impressive way. He talks about the original thinking behind the development of systems to measure profitability in retailing, quoting consulting firms (including McKenzies) who were developing ideas in the 1950s and 1960s.

"The whole approach now has a general title which is widely used in the more sophisticated circles," says Mike, "and that's DPP – Direct Product Profitability." He shows a transparency with these words on the overhead projector – very well prepared – to emphasise his point.

"There are very many variations on the same theme," he says, "and there have been many attempts to standardise.

But the general principles are much the same, whoever is using it."

I decide I'll interrupt, partly because I want to make a point and partly because I want to see how young Mike copes. As I do so, I see Jane give me an anxious glance – she is obviously concerned for her protégé and, if the rumours around Chapmans are true, her concern is probably felt at the personal level too. But who am I to pronounce on that, I think to myself, remembering once again how vulnerable my affair with Chris makes me feel.

"Are you suggesting that standardisation is a likely trend Mike? Because, if I was a retailer, I think I'd want to have my own system and not share it with others. Then it can be used more effectively in negotiation."

"Some retailers do think like that." I notice that he doesn't use my first name, he's not that confident after all I think. "Indeed Pathway have gone completely their own way and adopt a sort of 'Black Box' approach."

"Typical of them," intervenes Al, "they like to be different and they're always very mysterious."

Mike calmly takes back control. I'm impressed by the way he's dealt with the interruption.

"But most of the others are working along similar lines because, in their case, they've been following the lead set by the big suppliers Jane mentioned earlier. And, unlike Pathway, they see their future relationship with their suppliers as being mutually supportive rather than confrontational."

This is a good point and I also appreciate the fact that we've now got someone like Al to lead the sales function in these very different times. Henry was all right developing mutually supportive relationships if it involved lunch with his pals from way back. But sitting down with customers as partners working together on a complex profitability measurement system would have been totally beyond him and many of his old team.

Mike then continues and tells us that progress towards DPP depends very much on the product group. Detergents and toiletries are at the forefront whereas others, including, for example, frozen food products, are still hardly developed at all. This is partly because of the way that the system has been driven by certain suppliers but also because it is more difficult to do for some products than for others.

"Why is that Mike?" says Chris. "What is it that makes the difference?"

Again he copes with the interruption well. It is good to see young managers coming through in this way and it gives me some confidence about the future.

"Well, as you'll see Chris, the key variable which affects DPP is the space taken up in the store. With some products that varies a great deal and it's therefore much more important to measure it. In others there's not too much difference so it hasn't become such a big issue. The other important factor is the difficulty of measuring space taken up. It's much more difficult to measure space in, say, a frozen food cabinet or a delicatessen counter than it is on a shelf of shampoos where they're all tidily stacked."

Jane now joins in to support Mike but I think to myself that this man doesn't need any help.

"Perhaps we could let Mike show you the framework of the approach, then we can take questions with a bit more information to base them on," she says, looking pointedly at me.

Mike puts up a transparency which nicely summarises the whole idea of DPP.

I study this chart along with the others present but, like many diagrams of its kind, it sums up the concept but is rather difficult to transfer to practical application.

To Jane's obvious irritation, I ask another question.

"Could you just show us what that means in practice Mike? Maybe with a few numbers?"

Mike obviously doesn't share Jane's irritation because I've given him the ideal opening to move on to his next visual.

"Of course," he replies, "I know that top people at Chapmans always like to see the numbers so I've got a simple example to show you."

Though I know his comment was meant as a joke, it's an interesting reflection on how we're perceived. On

DIRECT PRODUCT PROFITABILITY

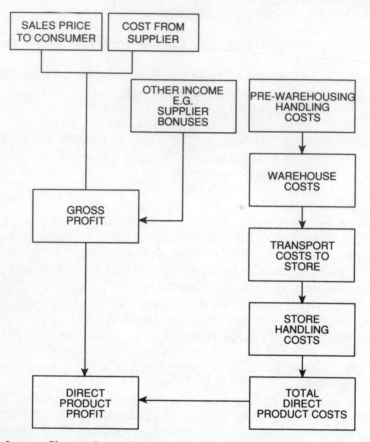

balance, I'm rather pleased if we are seen that way, as long as we don't become too financially driven. I make a mental note to talk to Chris about this. Maybe we should arrange for one of us to say something about it when we open the financial awareness course which Chris has been planning for some time and which starts next week. I want everyone to know that future success at Chapmans will, more than anything, be based on the right balance between financial and marketing issues.

Mike now puts up some numbers which help me to see the practical implications much more clearly. He says that companies like Valumart are now doing one of these evaluations for all the principal products they sell and they are constantly comparing them to each other.

DP PROFITABILITY CALCULATION

SALES PRICE TO CONSUMER		100
COST FROM SUPPLIER		75
GROSS PROFIT BEFORE OTHER INCOME		25
OTHER INCOME		5
GROSS PROFIT		30
PRE WAREHOUSE HANDLING COSTS	2	
WAREHOUSE COSTS	5	
TRANSPORT COSTS	3	
STORE HANDLING COSTS	11	21
DIRECT PRODUCT PROFIT		9

Chris is studying the figures carefully and, with her usual analytical approach, she is trying to find out what lies behind the figures.

"It must be a huge task getting out all those figures Mike. I can see that it's easy as far as Gross Profit because that's all from the invoices we send them but trying to split warehouse, transport and store costs by product must be a really complicated exercise?"

"I was thinking the same Chris," agrees Al. "There must be so many approximations and assumptions to work out any one of those costs that the result would be of very questionable value."

I'm a bit concerned about the way this discussion is

going because, surprisingly for two such normally positive people, Chris and Al are now being rather negative.

"Now come on you two," I say. "Chris, you once told me it was better to be approximately right than precisely wrong. I know that was in a financial accounting context but the principle is the same. It may be based on estimations but it's better than making decisions blind as retailers have been doing for years. And you could use just the same arguments about our Customer Profitability Statements which are also based on lots of estimates but they help us in our long-term thinking about customer relationships."

"And if I may build on that Phil," says Mike, now having the confidence to use my Christian name and smoothly using one of the Marketing Department's favourite clichés, "if customers are using them as part of their negotiations, which they are beginning to do more and more, we must understand them, however approximate they may be. I share some of the reservations you've expressed and sometimes they do get over elaborate but they seem to find it helps them in the same way as Customer Profitability Statements help your negotiators Al."

Chris is never one to mind losing an argument if the other view is well put over and I know that, on this subject, she would admit to be learning as much as any of us.

"OK Mike, I take your point," she says, "but can you give me some idea of how they go about collecting and calculating costs. Is there much known about this?"

"Oh yes Chris. The details of systems vary between individual retailers but the principles are much the same and have been well publicised due to suppliers like Mars and P & G. So it would not be impossible for us almost to replicate the computer program and do our own calculations. We'd have to invest quite a lot of time up front but that's what other manufacturers are doing."

I'm sure you'd like that young Mike, I think to myself rather cynically and probably rather unfairly, because that would make you very important to us. Anyone who specialises in this area will be a vital bridge between sales and marketing, something which is becoming more and more necessary in the current environment. And though communications have improved since Al was appointed, there's still a long way to go.

Mike is already moving on to tell us about the cost calculations.

"You don't need to go into the detail of the computer program to know that there are two key variables which have an impact on DPP," he says.

Then he brings out another transparency to make his point in big letters:

TWO KEY VARIABLES IN DPP

EASE OF HANDLING
SPACE TAKEN

"Get those right and your DPP will be better than your competitors," says Mike, "and that's where those who lead the way have been so clever. They developed special methods of packing and transporting their products – like easy stacking boxes or pallets – and they designed container sizes to minimise space taken up on the shelves of the warehouse and store. Then they introduced methods of calculating DPP to prove that the profit on their products is higher than competitors'. That's smooth marketing."

"That's why you've seen shampoo bottles getting narrower and taller," intervenes Jane, "because that way they take up less width on the shelf, get less costs allocated to them and therefore have a higher DPP than competitive products."

Chris has obviously now overcome her initial cynicism. She adds, "And those companies with the facility to unload mechanically from their trucks direct onto the customer's warehouse shelves will presumably also get lower cost allocations and higher DPP."

I think back to only two months ago when Chris and I rejected John Madden's capital proposal to install mechanical unloading gear on our older trucks. He couldn't produce a cash flow benefit and Al couldn't point to any problems in customer relationships which were being caused by our not having this gear. I criticised John for being technology driven – we can only afford to spend our capital budget on things which produce a measurable cash flow benefit, I told him. If John were here, I'm sure he'd say I told you so and I can tell from Chris's expression that she's thinking the same thing. Mike is now moving on to describe how the retailers have carried out work study exercises to measure warehouse handling time and I'm surprised how much detail they've gone into. They also measure in-store shelf stacking time so those companies who have easy to handle cases will benefit again. Apparently they allocate a lot of the store costs on the basis of space taken up which is probably as reasonable as any method.

Al is obviously still a bit cynical. I suspect he's been studying marginal costing during his MBA course and does not see the point of going to so much trouble to allocate store costs, like heating and management salaries, which are clearly fixed in relation to volume and product mix.

"I still think it's analysis paralysis," says Al. "It's not as if they'd save any of those costs if they changed the products they stock."

"Of course you're right about that Al," I reply, "but I think you're wrong in your general view for two reasons. I see more and more the distinction between two types of management accounting. You are thinking about the tactical approach, but what we're talking about here is strategic analysis. This is not about day-to-day changes in individual products but about the long-term implications of the product mix they handle and the impact on cost behaviour over a long period. For that you need to examine all costs, both fixed and variable."

Al looks a little surprised that I'm taking him on with this argument – these young men who take MBAs tend to think there's only one answer to a management problem. I then move on to make my other point.

"And secondly, you should remember that any management accounting information managers receive has to be valued according to its purpose and its benefit. If

Valumart and others like them find it helps them in their negotiations and in their long-term decision making, then it must be worth having. I agree that it has to be analytically sound but, from what Mike says, they've thought it through pretty well."

I see that Chris is looking at me with a rather far away and, unless I'm mistaken, adoring expression on her face. This makes me feel pretty good and I wonder what I've done to deserve it.

Mike then takes back control of the meeting. "There is one further factor I haven't mentioned which is used by the more sophisticated retailers," he says, "and that's the cost of stock-holding. It's the third key variable in the equation."

Chris is quick to see the two-edged aspect of this variable.

"You mean the interest charges for holding stock Mike?" He nods in reply. "Which will vary because of suppliers' different distribution systems and frequency of delivery?" He nods again.

Chris then continues. "But surely they can't take that into account without also bringing in the credit they take to fund the stock and that will also vary from supplier to supplier."

"Yes Chris," says Mike, "they evaluate a net stock figure and calculate interest on it at the average bank borrowing rate."

"By net stock you mean stock held less credit taken?" I ask, quite interested in this new factor which I hadn't previously thought of.

"Yes," says Mike, "and when I was at Valumart this meant a negative cost figure for some food suppliers because credit taken was more than average stock held."

They are getting quite sophisticated, I think to myself as Mike rounds off his presentation. We must take this into account in future when we try to negotiate terms of payment. Those with DPP systems will be particularly careful to evaluate the benefits of the credit they take from us. And I will have to be careful not to allow ABT's pressure for cash flow generation to let us go too far in restricting credit.

As I'm just going to leave the room at the end of the meeting, Chris asks me to stay behind with her. I hope she's remembered that our six month trial period is over and that now we've got to talk things through.

"Phil," she says, "I really think you are quite amazing."

I'm not sure quite how to respond to this but just say, "Oh yes?"

"That stuff about strategic management accounting – you put Al down so beautifully and it was absolutely right. It's exactly how my thinking has developed and I've built the split between the two types of management accounting into the design of the course we're doing next week. Part 1 is Operational Management Accounting – or tactical as you called it – and Part 2 is Strategic. I was wondering if you would say a few words to introduce it, on Wednesday morning in here?"

"Of course Chris, I'd love to. There are some points I'd like to make. Could you let me see the programme and the list of participants."

She agrees to do this and, as we're just packing up our papers, I say, "And Chris, we need to talk about us you know – the six months we gave ourselves is up now."

"Yes Phil I know. Can we leave it till next week? Maybe the Friday night after the course finishes? Shall I book Angelos?"

Angelos is an Italian Restaurant a few miles away from Chapmans, in a suburb where no-one knows us and there's little chance of our being seen. It's a rather special place for both of us.

I agree and want to talk more about things, in particular why she wants to leave it until next week. But I can see that she doesn't want to talk at all right now. It gives me an empty feeling in the pit of my stomach. I've an awful suspicion that the party's over and I'm not sure how I'm going to cope with it.

Chapter 18

I see all these expectant young faces in front of me. All the young managers of Chapmans, those who, if we can persuade them to stay with us, will have the future of the business in their hands. I see Mike McDivett, wearing his red braces again, displaying a well prepared and carefully balanced combination of confidence and enthusiasm.

I also see a few older and rather more cynical faces, mostly those still with us from the days before Richard took over and began to bring in new people to replace the old guard. Those who stayed are generally those who were more willing to accept the changes which Richard and I introduced but they still retain some of the old inertia. And attending a course like this is something which makes them feel threatened as it exposes them to competition from their younger, often brighter, colleagues.

Chris is standing up and welcoming everyone to the course while I'm sitting by the side waiting to say my piece. She's looking particularly attractive this morning – she's now lost the tousled look and has recently had her hair cut much shorter which suits her more than I expected.

Just as I'm sitting back and relaxing, enjoying the sound of that voice I know so well, she suddenly surprises and embarrasses me by starting to talk about me and our days at Lawrensons.

"There's no better way I can introduce this course than by telling you about the time I first met Philip Moorley.

He was Sales and Marketing Director at a company called Lawrensons which was part of Universal, based in the UK. I joined them from Universal's Head Office as a Management Accountant and I was just staggered by the lack of financial knowledge among all their managers, particularly those at senior level. And there was one who was worse than all the others and that was your Company President."

I look around the room and see that everyone is now listening intently to this story which is so familiar to me and which still feels as if it happened only yesterday. It even brings a bit of a lump to my throat because I've had this feeling all week that the whole thing between Chris and me is coming to an end. Having reconciled myself to the fact that we're probably finished at the personal level, I've also been thinking that she'll probably want to leave Chapmans too. And who could blame her? Someone with her potential is likely to move around a lot at this career stage, particularly in the US where people change jobs so regularly.

Having gained their attention, Chris makes sure she doesn't lose it by continuing the Lawrensons story and by using a bit of poetic licence to exaggerate the extent of my ignorance. Or have I just forgotten how bad I was?

"I can assure you that, however much you may lack knowledge in financial matters, Phil could have beaten you in spades. And he was the second most senior person in the whole company. Remember this was within Universal, a company which, like ABT, is driven to a large extent by financial objectives. So let's just think what this meant to someone like Phil and to the business. First of all, it made it very difficult for him to progress to a higher level, either at Universal or at any other big company. Secondly, it meant that decisions were being taken without full awareness of the financial implications. For example, new credit terms were being offered to customers without taking into account the impact on cash flow and interest costs. Cost budgets were exceeded without anyone looking at the effect on the bottom line of the business."

Though I'm slightly irritated and highly embarrassed by

the story, I can see how clever it is of Chris to tell it. It is so difficult to get people's attention at the beginning of an event like this. They usually take time to switch on to listening and they often read through the course papers while the first speaker is getting under way. But Chris has definitely got them hooked and she's also managing to communicate the course objectives in a most effective way. I glance down at these objectives which Chris sent to me last week:

- to understand the impact of decisions on the financial position of the business.

- to know more about the techniques of management accounting and the context in which they can be used.

- to communicate better with colleagues in the accounting function.

- to build general confidence and awareness in this important topic area.

Chris continues. "The other impact of having people at top level without financial knowledge was that full use was not being made of the analytical techniques which were available. In some cases this meant that decisions were being taken without any analysis at all, in others the wrong method was being used due to lack of understanding of the principles. You will see during this course that it is vital to use the tools and techniques we offer you in the right context, otherwise they can be counter-productive."

She now decides to sit down and make the atmosphere more informal, assuming a conversational, almost confiding tone – very effective as a way of keeping their attention. She certainly is exceptionally good in a training environment.

"Now you may think I'm being critical of the management at Lawrensons and of Phil in particular but really I'm not. Because the situation described is not that unusual in the UK and it's more common than you'd think over here, even if it may not always be admitted. And, in any case, the blame to a large extent lay with the accounting function who had not seen it as part of their job to communicate on financial matters with non-financial colleagues or to educate them about the principles which all managers needed to understand to be effective in that business. There was hardly any dialogue at all because the person who headed up the accounting function was a book-keeper at heart. He was steeped in financial accounting and this affected his attitude, his image and his own knowledge."

Chris now brings out a transparency to show more clearly what she means by financial accounting and how it differs from management accounting. By now this is familiar to me but it's useful to see it summarised so concisely.

TWO COMPLEMENTARY ELEMENTS OF BUSINESS ACCOUNTING

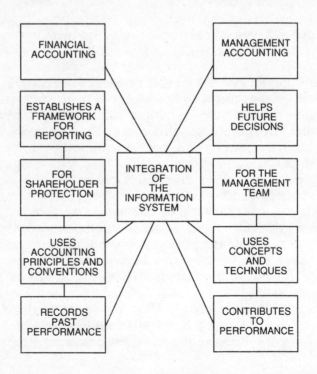

She now diverts away from the story of my transition from ignorance to enlightenment in order to explain this framework. She is careful not to disparage the financial accounting side, stressing its vital role in providing the framework of the Profit and Loss Account and Balance Sheet and its importance for both internal and external reporting. She emphasises how the shareholders must be protected by proper standards of information – otherwise management could, and probably would, take advantage. She mentions the key role of the external Auditors as guardians who ensure that the accounting rules are followed consistently, or at least most of the time (she refers briefly to one or two of the recent scandals which have caused Auditors to be sued for millions of dollars).

She also makes the vital point that there can be no good management accounting information about the future unless past actual data is properly recorded and while saying this, she points to the middle box of her visual which emphasises the need for proper integration of the two.

"This course," she says, "will be mainly concerned with management accounting because that's what you, the managers of Chapmans, need to understand, to use and to help us develop. Because management accounting, to be effective, must be constantly improved by the people who are in key management positions. And to do that we have to break down the mystique that surrounds the accounting profession and get you to see it as a service function like any other."

I can see the impact of what she's saying on the faces of those present. Accountants providing a service? Managers being expected to contribute to the development of management accounting? Though it may not be a surprise to those, like Mike McDivett, who are already closely involved with Chris and her team, I guess it is to those who are in areas without that advantage, particularly those on the production, research and distribution sides. And it's those to whom Chris is aiming this message.

"We're not going to ignore financial accounting completely because of the many areas of integration with management accounting. For instance we will study Profit and Loss Account and Balance Sheet principles at the beginning because they provide the framework for much of ABT and Chapmans' performance reporting."

She then moves on to make the distinction between the two types of management accounting which we discussed last week and which she has carefully built into her course design. I noticed this over the weekend when I was preparing for the introductory talk which I'm now waiting to deliver.

"There are many ways in which you can classify management accounting," she says, "based on the various concepts and techniques which are available. But there is one crucial distinction which becomes ever more clear to me as I develop my thinking on its use within the business. And this is the framework I've used when designing this course for you."

She puts up on the screen:

TWO TYPES OF MANAGEMENT ACCOUNTING

OPERATIONAL   - DAY TO DAY
                          - ROUTINE REPORTING

STRATEGIC   - LONG TERM
                          - SPECIAL ANALYSES

"You may wonder as the course progresses why we're spending so much time on this second category. You might even find it difficult to relate to this part of the course because the concepts are much less developed and there's much less technique to get your teeth into. But we think it's vital because Phil and I and the other VPs want you all to be involved in strategic planning in the future. We want you to be innovative and demanding about the special analyses you ask for from my department. The routine day-to-day reporting is already in place. We want you to build on the work we are now doing and improve our creativity in developing new ideas for financial information."

Some of the eyes in the audience open even more

widely. Creativity? They've probably heard stories of creative accounting but that was in a completely different and negative context. I hope these words from Chris are motivating them to learn and to apply their knowledge after the course. If not there must be something wrong with them. This is just what I should have had in my early Lawrensons days.

Just when I thought Chris had finished her recollections of my problems at Lawrensons, she returns to the story. I again feel a touch of nostalgia as she goes back to the day we first met – when I'd assumed that our new management accountant was a man, not a woman, called Chris Goodhart.

"I was sent in by Universal to try and improve their management accounting and I thought it would be easy. But the managers there were divided into two camps. Those who thought they knew it all and didn't want any help." She looks at me with a knowing smile and I know she's referring to John Appleby who was particularly obstructive in those early days. "And those who knew absolutely nothing about accounting and didn't think it particularly important. As I've mentioned, Philip was very much in the latter category but, fortunately, I was eventually able to convince him what good management accounting could do for him and the business."

Yes, I remember, it wasn't difficult to convince me. I was divorced, lonely, depressed and my career was going nowhere. Then along came this exquisite blonde vision and I was hooked. I would probably have believed anything she told me but the message she had for me was particularly well timed. I'd just been told by my boss that my career was unlikely to progress further in Universal unless I knew something about finance so I was pretty well motivated to learn.

"What was quite amazing about Phil and about many others in the same position, was that he had this mental block about accounting and financial matters. He lacked confidence. He thought it was more complicated than it really was. He was confused by all the mystique and the jargon. Yet, once we got over that problem, he began to show a quite exceptional flair for the subject, leading me, as he still does now, along new avenues, developing new ideas."

I feel I should not interrupt and say that it wasn't really that easy because Chris deserves some poetic licence this morning. But it wasn't easy. It took time, it took practice, it took determination and it took someone like Chris to work with me over a long period until it became natural. Until the words became more than words, became real measures of what was happening in the business. Then I was able to work on my own, looking at our customers' financial results, analysing our internal information with new enthusiasm and, finally, becoming confident enough to request special analyses which weren't being produced on a routine basis. Then I went on a Universal course to find that other managers were struggling to understand what now came naturally to me. How good it felt when I was actually able to help them!

"So when, in the future, you work closely with Philip, you will be struck by his aptitude for numbers, his ability to spot what is happening in the business from a few key indicators, his knowledge (ˆ management accounting concepts and his constant drive to develop new ways of presenting information. Just remember that this is the result of a long learning curve which he's still travelling along and also frequently taking me with him. For, despite my accounting qualification and my MBA, I'm still learning all the time from Phil, from the other VPs, from people like Mike McDivett here who's been helping us with new ideas on costing in the retail business. That's what good management accounting is about. It's about dialogue, learning from each other, constantly searching for improvement in information as the business changes and develops. And you are all capable of it. My story about Phil should prove that to you."

I see the enthusiasm showing on her face and coming through to everyone as she raises her voice to draw her introduction to an end. There's a silence as everyone looks at her, rather like the way a cinema audience stays quiet for a few moments after a thought-provoking film.

Is she being sycophantic I wonder? All that did seem a bit over the top because after all, what I do is mainly common sense. But no, that's not Chris's way and, in any case, she knows she doesn't have to impress me. She must mean it, she really rates my financial expertise. I'm curious to know if she still rates me in other ways, but I guess I won't find that out until Friday evening.

Chris has sat down and is looking towards me, obviously now expecting me to do my thing. This takes me by surprise because I thought she was going to introduce me but obviously not. I get up to play my part in setting the right context for the course.

"I'm not quite sure how I can follow that," I say. "I didn't know Chris was going to go back to our old days in the UK so I'm not really prepared to respond. Except to say that she's exaggerated enormously of course." I turn round and smile at her, showing others in the room that I don't really mind her revealing my past problems. "But the essential message she put over is absolutely right. I had a mental block about financial information. I was numerate, I could take away numbers brilliantly when I was playing darts but somehow I felt that accounting was so complex that only the accountants could understand it. So, if you can develop confidence in the way that I did, you will become comfortable with financial information – but you'll have to work at it. Unlike me, you've got the advantage of a course like this at an early stage of your career, instigated by accounting colleagues who really want to help you understand what they do and why they do it. Based on my experience of many accountants I've heard about and come across, you're very lucky to have Chris and her people helping you in this way."

I then go through the objectives of the course as Chris requested and reinforce many of the points that she made earlier. I can feel their interest waning: I can't pretend to have the same talent for this kind of communication as Chris. I feel pleased that I prepared some visuals over the weekend because that will take some of the pressure off me. I've deliberately kept them from Chris because I'm rather proud of them and want them to be a surprise to her. I also fear that maybe she'd want me to change them if they don't quite fit into her way of thinking about the course. And I don't want to change them because they contain messages which I want these managers to take in before they begin to learn about this difficult subject.   I know from my own problems and experiences in the past, that it is vital to have a framework in which to fit all the concepts and techniques which will be thrown at them during the next three days.   Otherwise it becomes a jumble that is. difficult to reconcile to the day-to-day responsibilities of managing a complex business like Chapmans.

I steal a sideways look at Chris as I draw out the results of my weekend work.

"Chris has already mentioned that vital split between operational and strategic management accounting information. I've developed a framework here which reflects my own experience and which should help you to see how it all fits together and relates to the way we make decisions in Chapmans."

I then pull out one of the transparencies I've prepared and put it on the OHP.

I then try to explain the thinking behind this framework.

"Now I don't expect you to be able to relate to this fully yet but, as you deal with these issues during the course, I want you to refer back to it and see how all the concepts and techniques relate together. I haven't developed this as some abstract concept. I've tried to base it on what we actually do at Chapmans."

I don't tell them how long it took, how many attempts I had at it, how many lines were going from box to box until I finally understood how complex the integration between the various types of decision really is.

"What struck me as I developed this framework was how strong are the relationships between the various techniques and how they integrate.   Apart from investment and disinvestment decisions – which I've included at the top and which are usually fairly self-contained projects – the other concepts and techniques all combine together as a powerful array of tools which help you to make complex and integrated decisions. And, of course, investment

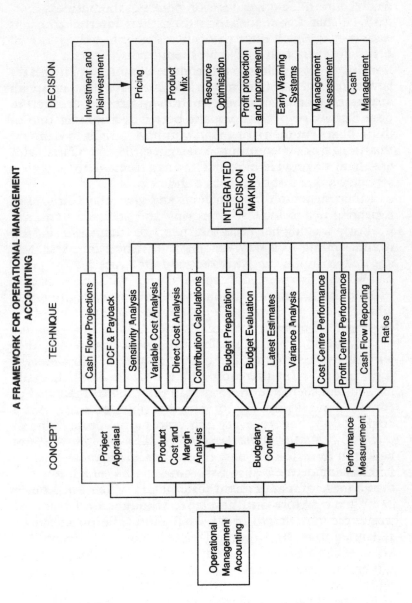

A FRAMEWORK FOR OPERATIONAL MANAGEMENT ACCOUNTING

CONCEPT

Operational Management Accounting

- Project Appraisal
- Product Cost and Margin Analysis
- Budgetary Control
- Performance Measurement

TECHNIQUE

- Cash Flow Projections
- DCF & Payback
- Sensitivity Analysis
- Variable Cost Analysis
- Direct Cost Analysis
- Contribution Calculations
- Budget Preparation
- Budget Evaluation
- Latest Estimates
- Variance Analysis
- Cost Centre Performance
- Profit Centre Performance
- Cash Flow Reporting
- Ratios

INTEGRATED DECISION MAKING

DECISION

- Investment and Disinvestment
- Pricing
- Product Mix
- Resource Optimisation
- Profit protection and improvement
- Early Warning Systems
- Management Assessment
- Cash Management

projects, though often treated as self-contained decisions, will feed in to the other decision points of the business."

I see that I've managed to gain their interest and it is encouraging that a number of them begin to write it down. I reassure them that I will give them a copy.

"So, as you talk about product costing or budgetary control or ratios, remember that they are all part of an integrated management information system which must, to be effective, help you to make better decisions in one of those boxes on the right. And you have a right to demand this from your accounting colleagues who, as Chris said, are there to provide all of us in management roles with a service which must be effective and helpful."

I then switch off the projector and glance at Chris. I'm expecting her to look disapproving and at first I think she is. She's shaking her head but then I see that she's shaking it and smiling in a way that indicates she's impressed. I decide to continue with my second framework.

"When I first started to come to grips with the subject, I used to think that operational management accounting was what it was all about. You needed a set of product costings, a budgetary control system, good performance measures and a procedure for investment appraisal. And, with Chris's support, we soon got those into place at Lawrensons. But then something happened which made me see that there's more to it than that. Chris managed to convince me, as the Director responsible for sales, that I ought to have reports every half year, on the profitability of our dealings with major customers, the sort that those of you from the sales side now receive at Chapmans.

"This made me realise two things. First of all, this was a vital piece of management information which I had never been given before and had never thought to ask for. I wondered how much more useful information could be generated if we sat down and thought about it. Secondly I knew that this was different information – longer-term rather than short-term, occasional rather than frequent, STRATEGIC rather than OPERATIONAL.

"In fact it was dangerous to use it in an operational context because you could make decisions which would be against the interests of the business. We found that the customer profitability statements were useful to help us develop a long-term strategy, not to push us into hasty tactical ploys to improve profitability.

"So since I've been at Chapmans, and particularly since Chris came, I've been seeing more and more the benefits of Strategic Management Accounting which will be covered in Part 2 of this course which you will be doing in a few weeks' time. As Chris said, this is where you can make the greatest contribution by giving us lots of new ideas, so I've developed a similar framework to help you."

"Now when you get the detailed programme for the second part of the course, you'll see that Chris is going to cover all these areas, many of which I've only been introduced to over the last twelve months or so. The various approaches – and they are better seen as approaches to analysis rather than the more complete techniques which you get on the operational side – have come from various sources. Some have come from Chris, some from us on the management side and a lot from the ABT Internal Auditors who came in a while ago. At times it seemed as if new approaches and concepts were being rained on me from all sides and I wasn't quite sure how it all fitted together. I'm still not completely sure but drawing out this framework helped me to think more clearly and I hope it helps you too. One thing you will note again is that, as on the operational side, it is all very complex and integrated into the strategic management of the business. But I'm convinced that, if we continue to develop this part of our management information system with your help, we will be gaining a very substantial competitive edge."

I can see from the expressions on their faces that I've regained their interest and this pleases me a lot. I feel I should quickly move on to make my two final points before handing back to Chris to start the course proper.

"Now there's something I want to make clear to all of you before you start on this course," I say, "and it's this. You will never achieve the right level of learning to satisfy me and I hope yourselves, if you regard this as just a 'one-

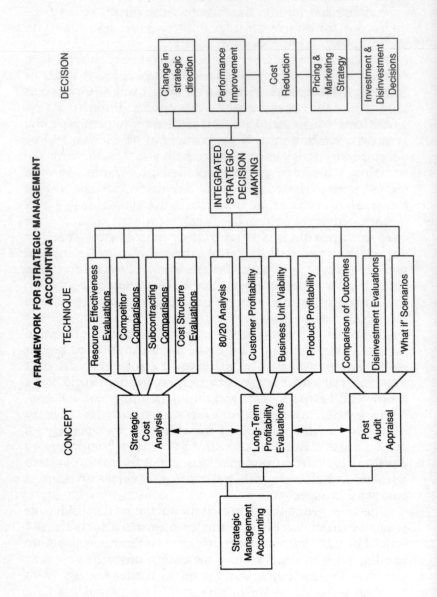

A FRAMEWORK FOR STRATEGIC MANAGEMENT ACCOUNTING

off' event. The secret of success is PRACTICE.''

I write this up on the flipchart in big letters to re-emphasise the point.

"If you go away on Friday afternoon and do nothing to apply what you've learnt, you'll have forgotten it all within weeks. I expect you to set yourselves tasks, individually or in groups, which ensure that you keep using the concepts and the techniques in real situations. This might be something of personal interest outside Chapmans – like analysing the accounts of a company in which you maybe want to buy stock – or working on a particular internal project with Chris or one of her team. From my own personal experience, it was only when I began to use financial information on my own in this way that it really began to stick.''

Before I make my final point, I bring out the other transparency which I prepared over the weekend, much to the irritation of Jean as I worked late on Sunday evening. But I'm very pleased with the result, even though I'm uncertain whether Chris will be entirely happy with the message.

"I still have one final message which I feel I must put to you. There are certain dangers of running a course like this and, as your Company President, I have to guard against them. In particular I want you all to see your knowledge of financial measures and techniques in the right context. They are not everything and the various approaches you use must be balanced against other factors in the business, however difficult and intangible these may be. In fact I would argue that one of the key tasks of a manager is to achieve that balance consistently. You must look at financial information and use it as a support to your decisions – you must not hide behind it and avoid your responsibilities for management judgement. Equally you must not ignore it and take decisions without weighing up the financial implications. This matrix might help you to see what I'm getting at and apply the course content with the right balance.''

I put up my transparency on the screen.

MATRIX OF DECISION MAKING

AUTOCRATIC

ANALYTICAL ———————————— VISIONARY

CONSULTATIVE

"Now I think that Richard, my predecessor whom most of you have met, would admit to being top right. His style of decision making was fairly top down and he was supported in this by Chris's predecessor as CFO who did not have the same desire to share financial information with the management team. And that was right for Chapmans at the time because Richard needed to bring about some radical changes and he was a brilliantly intuitive manager, particularly when starting the marketing initiatives which are now bearing fruit for us."

I can feel interest and even some warmth coming back from the faces in front of me. I guess they're not used to someone at my level being as open as this in public but I've decided that this is the style which is needed if Chapmans is to move to the next stage of its development. And this is the ideal forum to make this clear to everyone.

"The problem about this was that the techniques of financial evaluation were not that rigorous but Richard's brilliance was able to overcome this. But now Richard's gone and something else has changed – we are part of ABT. We are also moving to an era where our decision making has to be more consultative because I'm not a marketing genius like Richard. Thus we have to move downwards and to the left on my matrix. We can't just move downwards to the bottom right-hand corner because we will all make the wrong judgements without the support of financial evaluations."

I take a sideways look at Chris to see how she's taking this and I'm slightly disconcerted to find that she's staring straight at me with that same look of wonderment which I saw at the meeting on DPP last week. I recall again those words she uttered at Heathrow when she first went to the States four years ago. "I thought you were fantastic from the first time I saw you." Maybe I'm letting my chronic lack of self-confidence make me too pessimistic – maybe she really does love me. Maybe she will be prepared to make the full commitment we discussed during that wonderful weekend in Washington.

"But the danger is," I continue, fighting to keep my concentration, "that we fall into the trap of descending too far into the bottom left-hand corner – the ANALYSIS PARALYSIS syndrome." I now put an overlay on top of the transparency.

MATRIX OF DECISION MAKING

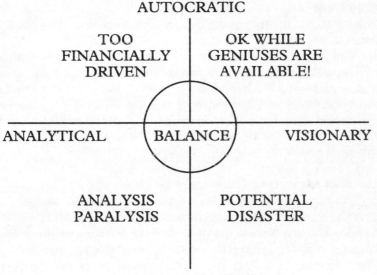

"There would also be a problem if the top left corner applied – if I, or ABT, allowed the business to become too financially driven from the top. When I was at Universal I used to feel that the financial pressures within that Group created that situation and I even thought that ABT was like that at first."

I now point to the middle of the matrix. "But I'm now convinced that ABT, your VPs and all of you can work together to achieve the necessary BALANCE which I think is essential for Chapmans at this stage of its corporate life. We give you strategic direction from the top, we encourage you to put forward proposals, we ask you to analyse decisions, we get you to submit them to us, we challenge your assumptions, we maybe refer your proposals back for further analysis. That's the balance between autocratic and consultative on the vertical axis.

The mid point of the analytical/visionary axis indicates that, whoever makes the final judgement – and it could be me or you depending on the scale of the decision – looks at the financial as well as the wider, long-term, strategic, maybe intangible issues before making a balanced judgement one way or the other."

I now get up to emphasise the importance of my final sentence.

"And I can assure you all that, though I may, from now on, be looking for those of you who have the right grasp of financial matters when deciding who will take on wider responsibilities in Chapmans, I will be looking even more for those who have the courage to take decisions and achieve this difficult but essential balance. Enjoy your course."

There's a respectful silence as I sit down and Chris now moves over to where I was standing.

"Perhaps we should take a five minute break before we start the course content. Back at 9.45 am."

I look at my watch and see that I've been speaking for 30 minutes, far longer than I'd intended. I apologise to Chris for this as she gets her material together for the first part of the course.

She turns round to face me. "Phil – you don't need to apologise, you idiot. That was fantastic. I don't believe there's a Company President in the whole of the Western world who would start a course like that. Who would develop those special frameworks."

"Did you like them?" I say, fishing pathetically for compliments.

"Like them? They were brilliant – I just felt guilty that I hadn't produced them myself. Can I hang on to them because I'd like to use them from time to time as the course progresses?"

I agree to this and say, "Have a good course," as I walk out of the room. "If I don't see you before, Angelos at 8 o'clock on Friday," I whisper as she comes to the door with me.

"Sure Phil," she replies, "I hadn't forgotten."

I return to my office with a sense of elation which it is difficult to justify rationally. Maybe it's because I feel that, even if I find out on Friday that I haven't got Christine's love any more, I have gained her respect. And somehow, on this particular morning, this seems to be more important.

Chapter 19

We're sitting at our usual table in the far corner of Angelos restaurant. When you're having an illicit affair, you never sit by the window. Chris is looking quite lovely tonight, no longer the pretty, doll-like attractiveness of her Lawrensons days - she is now undoubtedly a beautiful woman by any standards. Since I've known her she seems to have improved with age and maturity and, when I'm with her like this, all I want is be with her always, whatever the consequences for my career or my family.

My suspicions that this is not what she wants are confirmed as she tries to change the subject whenever I start to talk about our future. She tells me at great length about the course which she obviously enjoyed enormously and which, I had already heard from other sources, was an unqualified success. Then she starts to talk about her plans to develop a regular post-audit system for all new investments and it's then that I decide that I've had enough.

"Chris," I say, "we've come here to talk about us, to make a decision about our future and, I'm sorry, but I find it unreal to talk about anything else."

"OK Phil. I'm sorry but I guess I'm trying to delay what I have to say to you." She stops talking, looks down, then up into my eyes and says, "Because you're not going to like it."

My heart seems to stop for a moment. With those few

simple but devastating words my suspicions are confirmed with awful certainty.

Just then the waiter arrives to take our order and I just can't concentrate on the menu. I order lasagne because I can do that without thinking. We put down our menus and I ask the question which has been nagging away at me these last few weeks.

"Is it someone else?"

"Yes Phil, I'm afraid it is."

"Someone I know?"

"Yes, you remember the Internal Auditors."

"Oh no Chris not that awful poseur Palmer." I then realise how jealous and vindictive that sounds and say, "I'm sorry I shouldn't have said that."

"It doesn't matter Phil, because I thought Bob Palmer was an awful poseur too. It's not him I'm in love with, it's Steve - don't you remember Steve?"

I sit back in my chair and think about Steve. Small, boyish, academic looking, very bright I must admit but surely not Chris's type. I guess she must have read my mind because she says, "You never did understand what attracts a woman Phil or at least what attracts me. I remember you were jealous of Martyn Ames at Lawrensons, another blonde Adonis whom you assumed I would be drooling over. What attracted me about you was not your looks, it was your dynamism, your energy, your determination to overcome your problems at Lawrensons and, I'm sure it will surprise you to know, the power and creativity of your mind."

"So why Steve?"

"Because he has all those things too, though with a lot less maturity so far. And I'm sorry but I really do love him, like I never have before. It just sort of happened."

"So you've been having an affair with him? For how long?"

"We haven't been having an affair Phil. I told him that wasn't possible until I'd told you. And it won't just be an affair, we'll be getting married fairly soon."

The awful finality of that statement seems to bring me back to earth. There's no point in arguing, it really is over.

And I have to ask the other question which follows from that.

"Does that mean you'll be leaving Chapmans too?"

"It doesn't on its own Phil. I think we could both be rational and adult enough not to let this get in the way of our jobs."

I think to myself that I don't feel at all rational or adult but I decide not to say so.

She carries on with her second bombshell.

"But I want to leave for different reasons. I've decided I don't want to do this kind of job anymore. I want to make a career change."

"To do what Chris?" I ask, hardly knowing what to expect.

"Management education Phil. It's something I enjoy more than I can tell you. This course this week gave me more reward than anything I've ever done before. I just love helping other people to understand things. You must have noticed that."

Yes, of course I've noticed and I've thought to myself many times that she would be brilliant in that kind of role. But, selfishly thinking of the impact on Chapmans, the first question to come to my mind is when this is all going to happen.

"Don't worry Phil, I'm not going to rush. I'll find you a successor as I did at Lawrensons and I'll make sure there's a good handover period."

"But where are you going Chris? One of the Business Schools?"

"I'm going back to the UK to go into partnership with two men who are just leaving one of the Business Schools to start on their own. I've known one of them well since University. They want me to manage their financial training business. When I mentioned it to Steve, he said he's always wanted to work in the UK so he'll be applying to ABT for a transfer. I guess it's all somehow come together for us."

"Isn't management training a very competitive business?"

"Not really Phil. We're going to concentrate on tailor-made courses and we think there's a fantastic market potential. The Business Schools tend to dominate but they have a very academic approach and they're also very expensive. We believe we can undercut them, produce a better product and still make a lot of money."

"I'm sure you will Chris but I do wish you'd told me before."

"Phil, Steve and I only made up our minds yesterday evening. I didn't want to worry you if it was not likely to happen and there was an awful lot to sort out, including Steve's career. Please try to understand."

I reach across the table and take her hand.

"Chris," I say, "I can't say I'm surprised at either of your decisions but it won't stop me missing you. I honestly have enjoyed every moment of our time together, at work and outside. You are very special to me."

She smiles tenderly and our eyes meet, only to be interrupted by the arrival of our first course. We sit back to receive Angelo's best antipasta and the tender moment has gone. I have to accept that now it really is over and I must get on with my life.

Two hours later I open my front door and let myself in. As I walk through the lobby I look around and see what a wonderful home I have. I think to myself that I haven't really looked at it properly for many months. Home has been a place where I've called in occasionally and gone through the motions of life with my family. All my energy and my emotions have been diverted towards Chris and Chapmans. But now I've got to rebuild my family life. Somehow it's a relief to know that this is now my only option if I am to avoid once again the awful loneliness of living on my own.

As I walk into the lounge, I see Jean sitting there watching a video. She looks lovely and this is also something I notice for the first time in a long time. I suddenly comprehend the enormity of what I've been doing to her and it hits me very hard. I've not really noticed her at all - I've pecked her on the cheek in the morning to say goodbye and I've sometimes discussed our children's progress at school. But I've not really been communicating with her at all.

I know instantly that, if there's going to be any chance of getting back together again and doing more than go through the motions, I have to tell her the truth, the complete truth, nothing else will do. I sit down beside her on the settee. I put my arm around her and tell her what I've been doing these last eight months or so, how I've let her down, how I've abused her loyalty and her trust after she gave me a second chance and agreed to marry me again. I consider lying about Chris's decision to ditch me and pretend that it was my idea but I decide to be completely honest.

She's silent for a while and then says, "You didn't really need to tell me Phil. I've had a fairly good idea what was going on and it was obvious who it would be. And I would probably have left you by now but for one thing."

"One thing?"

"Yes love. You see I've had an affair too so maybe I understand a bit more about what happened to you and Chris and how difficult it can be to resist."

Suddenly my world's turned upside down. Jean, the ultimate loyal person, the faithful wife, the one whom I would have trusted more than anyone, has had an affair. Though I have no right to, I feel let down and resentful. I can't help asking the question that's burning in my mind.

"Who with Jean, please tell me."

"It was in England last year Phil. It was absolutely crazy and you're going to be furious when you know who."

"Jean, please tell me."

"It was Richard, Phil. I'm sorry."

Half an hour later we're having a drink to relax and discuss the rebuilding of our future together. We've both been as honest and open as we can be and I feel I can ask the question that's still bugging me since I heard this devastating news.

"Did you love him Jean?"

"I think so Phil."

"And did you think of leaving me?"

"We talked about it Phil. Only a few weeks ago. But there is a problem."

"The children?"

"No Phil. I would have taken them with me if necessary."

"What then?"

She gets up and stands sideways on, facing the window, wearing a silk dressing gown tied tightly around her. She turns her head towards me.

"Don't you know Phil? You really have been somewhere else these last few months. Can't you see you idiot, I'm four months pregnant, that's the bottom line."

I thought I'd taken all the shocks I could take today. I look at my wife and don't have to ask that final, obvious question which is driving me crazy.

"Don't worry darling. It's yours. Don't you think it's wonderful?"

I look back at her and remember why I love her and why I'll always come back to her.

"Yes, of course darling, absolutely wonderful," I reply.

As we go to bed to make yet another new start, I wonder if deep down I really believe it.

Index

Management Training Partnership

Since its formation in 1987, MTP has grown rapidly to become the largest UK provider of tailored management training outside the business schools. Indeed for many of its major company clients it has become a preferable high value alternative to traditional academic programmes.

The main areas of focus are:

- finance and management accounting
- marketing
- human resource management
- business management programmes which integrate these core topics within tailored, innovative course designs.

The client list is evidence of the success which MTP has achieved and includes:

- Unilever
- Marks & Spencer
- British Airways
- Smith Kline Beecham

The innovative and practical nature of this book – written by one of MTP's founding partners – is a good example of our ability to provide user-friendly and effective learning for your managers.

For further information, please contact:

Alan Warner
Management Training Partnership plc
3 Prebendal Court
Oxford Road
Aylesbury
Bucks   HP19 3EY
England

Telephone: 0296 23474   Facsimile: 0296 393879

Becoming the Best

How to Gain Company-wide Commitment to Total Quality

Barry Popplewell and Alan Wildsmith

How could it happen in a buoyant market? New products, lots of orders, and yet no profit – a big fat ZERO. The opportunity had been there – and he'd blown it. As the story unfolds Neil begins to understand the problem.

Quality is the key – not just product quality but total quality. "If everybody was the best at what they do," he thought " then this would be one hell of a company." So that's what he sets out to do – become the best. How he conceives his idea, translates it into practice, cajoles and carries his employees with him, is all in this fascinating book.

Contents

"The day had started bad. It couldn't get any worse."; "Facts...the bright stepping stones of logic."; "No problem's too big. What it needs is a big solution, and the will to do it."; "What it means is, you're not in control."; "One common aim for everybody."; "The organization was rife with rumour."; "He didn't want a navigation officer, he wanted a bomb-disposal squad."; "Improve the whole organization, everybody, everywhere. Impossible?"; "This whole organization is going to be turned upside down."; "Everybody is a supplier and a customer."; "Enthusiasm, a sense of purpose, you don't generate those by pushing a piece of paper under somebody's nose."; "Basic questions like 'Do you know who your customers are?'"; "No more red-label orders, no panics. What a sweet life."; "Best in the world applies to people, not things."; "Hold on to your vision. Stay with it". Epilogue.

1988   156 pages   0 566 02798 4 Hardback   0 566 02877 8 Paperback

Gower

The Bottom Line

Practical Financial Management in Business

Alan Warner

A Gower Novel

In this remarkable book Alan Warner uses the power of romantic fiction
to explain the key concepts of business finance. By creating a believable
set of characters and a compelling story he has provided an easy and
enjoyable way to understand balance sheets, budgeting, marginal costing,
investment appraisal, profit maximization, performance measurement
and other modern accounting techniques.

The story concerns Phil Moorley, Sales and Marketing Director of
Lawrence & Sons, and his relationship with Christine Goodhart, the
management accountant imposed on the company by its conglomerate
owners. Moorley's big professional weakness is his lack of financial
knowledge, but with Chris' help he begins to learn - and the reader
learns with him. In the process his feelings for Chris grow stronger - but
will she ever be willing to offer him more than friendship and tutorials?
After a number of crises, Moorley begins to prepare himself for a more
ambitious role. Then fate steps in, and both his business and personal
life take a swift new turn.

The Bottom Line is as far from a conventional textbook as can be
imagined. Its readability and its business setting combine to make it the
best possible introduction to business finance for the non-accountant.

1988   231 pages   0 566 07265 3 Hardback   0 566 07480 X Paperback

The Focused Business Plan

Vandenburghs Chartered Accountants

The Focused Business Plan is a highly practical and readable guide to evaluating a business from the vantage points of sales/costs/cash and assimilating that information into a clearly defined business strategy. It guides you through the initial stages of why the business plan is essential and who should prepare it, to establishing basic information, concentrating on specific areas of the plan and eventually, to who the users are and how the plan should best be presented to them. Model plans are used to illustrate the various stages.

Contents

1992   186 pages   0 566 07286 6

Gower

The Goal
Beating the Competition
Second Edition

Eliyahu M Goldratt and Jeff Cox

Written in a fast-paced thriller style, *The Goal* is the gripping novel which is transforming management thinking throughout the Western world.

Alex Rogo is a harried plant manager working ever more desperately to try to improve performance. His factory is rapidly heading for disaster. So is his marriage. He has ninety days to save his plant - or it will be closed by corporate HQ, with hundreds of job losses. It takes a chance meeting with a colleague from student days - Jonah - to help him break out of conventional ways of thinking to see what needs to be done.

The story of Alex's fight to save his plant is more than compulsive reading. It contains a serious message for all managers in industry and explains the ideas which underlie the Theory of Constraints (TOC) developed by Eli Goldratt - the author described by Fortune as 'a guru to industry' and by Businessweek as a 'genius'.

As a result of the phenomenal and continuing success of *The Goal*, there has been growing demand for a follow-up. Eliyahu Goldratt has now written ten further chapters which continues the story of Alex Rogo as he makes the transition from Plant Manager to Divisional Manager. Having achieved the turnround of his plant, Alex now attempts to apply all that Jonah has taught him, not to crisis management, but to ongoing improvement.

These new chapters reinforce the thinking process utilised in the first edition of *The Goal* and apply them to a wider management context with the aim of stimulating readers into using the technique in their own environment.

| 1993 | 352 pages | 0 566 07417 6 Hardback | 0 566 07418 4 Paperback |

Gower

Managing Mergers and Acquisitions

A Practical Guide to Managing Domestic and Cross Border Company Integration

Ann McDonagh Bengtsson

Acquiring may be more fun than managing, but in the 1990s businesses cannot afford to buy companies then sub-optimize their investment through shoddy management. And it is never too late to repair past mistakes. Nobody knows better than practitioners what makes mergers and acquisitions work or how it feels to face furious shareholders at the AGM when they do not. This is the real world of M&As – success, failure and above all, accountability. Top European managers uninhibitedly contribute ideas, reflections and experience. Their practical views are synthesised by a European management consultant into a highly readable aid to successful management of M&As. Practical guidelines and illustrative comments applicable to all acquisitions are complemented by a separate section on cross border deals. International target selection, negotiation, cultural awareness and the realities of doing business in risky places are among the topics covered. Case studies in the words of four presidents, one vice-president and three senior directors from six contrasting business heritages add insight into M&A policy and practice in some of Europe's most interesting companies.

Contents

Acknowledgements; Introduction; Part One: Preparation, Principles and Practice; Section A – Preparing for success; Section B – Making the merger work; Section C – Managing people – a key factor; Section D – Consolidation; Part Two: Cross Border Acquisitions; Part Three: Case Studies; Appendices.

1992   192 pages   0 566 07304 8

Gower

The Meaning of Company Accounts

Fifth Edition

Walter Reid and D R Myddelton

The Meaning of Company Accounts first appeared in 1971 and quickly achieved recognition among managers, financial and non-financial alike. Its "workbook" approach stems from the need for a treatment of financial accounting practice which readers at differing levels of knowledge can tailor individually to their learning requirements. The authors, both of them distinguished teachers of finance and accounting, adopt programmed learning techniques within a firmly structured text in order to provide for a wide variety of readers' needs. At controlled points the reader is invited to work through examples and write into the workbook his or her solutions to problems. These active responses both reinforce what has been learned and extend the reader's experience and skill in using, preparing and interpreting company accounts.

For this fifth edition, the authors have revised their text to reflect recent developments, including new accounting standards and changes in company law. They have added material on brands, and an appendix of photocopiable formats covering financial ratios, segment analysis and cash/funds flow.

Contents

The background and structure of company accounts • Analysing company accounts • Recording business transactions • Measuring profit or loss • Fixed assets and depreciation • Cash flow statements • Company taxation • Capital structure • Group accounts • International accounting • Inflation accounting • Interpreting company accounts • Appendices • Solutions • Index.

1992   376 pages   0 566 07349 8 Hardback   0 566 07350 1 Paperback

The Noah Project
The Secrets of Practical Project Management

Ralph L Kliem and Irwin S Ludin

This book is a novelization of project management. The characters and events are fictitious; however the techniques, tools, and circumstances described in each chapter are real for just about every project in any environment, from technical to financial. The scenes explain project management from the vantage point of David Michaels, a young executive working for a private zoo. He must manage the dismantling of the zoo through to a successful conclusion. He has little idea how to go about such a task until he meets Noah...

David encounters common pitfalls such as failure to achieve targets on time, budgeting restrictions, an already unreasonable schedule cut back even further, and of course the inevitable staff conflict. In his moments of crisis Noah forces David to think for himself, thereby encouraging the reader to do the same.

The authors have chosen the setting intentionally to show how anyone in any organization can put the methods and concepts of project management to use. The book also includes a 'model' project manual which can be adapted easily to the reader's own projects. Anyone looking for an enjoyable introduction to the secrets of project management will find it in *The Noah Project*.

1993   208 pages   0 566 07439 7

Gower

Learning Resources